Kaplan Publishing are constantly finding new
ways to make a difference to your
exciting online resources really do
different to students looking for exam success.

This book comes with free MyKaplan online resources so that
you can study anytime, anywhere. **This free online resource is
not sold separately and is included in the price of the book.**

Having purchased this book, you have access to the following online study materials:

CONTENT	AAT	
	Text	Kit
Electronic version of the book	✓	✓
Progress tests with instant answers	✓	
Mock assessments online	✓	✓
Material updates	✓	✓

How to access your online resources

Kaplan Financial students will already have a MyKaplan account and these extra resources will be available to
you online. You do not need to register again, as this process was completed when you enrolled. If you are having
problems accessing online materials, please ask your course administrator.

If you are not studying with Kaplan and did not purchase your book via a Kaplan website, to unlock your extra online
resources please go to www.mykaplan.co.uk/addabook (even if you have set up an account and registered books
previously). You will then need to enter the ISBN number (on the title page and back cover) and the unique pass key
number contained in the scratch panel below to gain access. You will also be required to enter additional information
during this process to set up or confirm your account details.

If you purchased through Kaplan Flexible Learning or via the Kaplan Publishing website you will automatically receive
an e-mail invitation to MyKaplan. Please register your details using this email to gain access to your content. If you do
not receive the e-mail or book content, please contact Kaplan Publishing.

Your Code and Information

This code can only be used once for the registration of one book online. This registration and your online content will
expire when the final sittings for the examinations covered by this book have taken place. Please allow one hour from
the time you submit your book details for us to process your request.

Please scratch the film to access your MyKaplan code.

Please be aware that this code is case-sensitive and you will need to include the dashes
within the passcode, but not when entering the ISBN. For further technical support,
please visit www.MyKaplan.co.uk

USING ACCOUNTING SOFTWARE

STUDY TEXT

Qualifications and Credit Framework

AQ2016

This Study Text supports study for the following AAT qualifications:

AAT Foundation Certificate in Accounting – Level 2

AAT Foundation Diploma in Accounting and Business – Level 2

AAT Foundation Certificate in Bookkeeping – Level 2

AAT Foundation Award in Accounting Software – Level 2

AAT Level 2 Award in Accounting Skills to Run Your Business

AAT Foundation Certificate in Accounting at SCQF Level 5

British Library Cataloguing-in-Publication Data

A catalogue record for this book is available from the British Library.

Published by
Kaplan Publishing UK
Unit 2, The Business Centre
Molly Millars Lane
Wokingham
Berkshire
RG41 2QZ

ISBN: 978-1-78740-262-1

Printed and bound in Great Britain

We are grateful to Sage (UK) Limited for their support in the preparation of this Text.

CONTENTS

Introduction   P.5

Unit guide   P.6

The assessment   P.11

Study skills   P.12

STUDY TEXT

Chapter   *Page No.*

1   An introduction to computerised accounting   1

2   Signing up to Sage Business Cloud Accounting   9

3   Setting up your company   11

4   Navigating Sage Business Cloud Accounting   19

5   Setting up your suppliers' details   29

6   Setting up your customers' details   43

7   The nominal ledger   55

8   Entering transactions   69

9   Journals   109

10   Bank reconciliation   113

11   Useful reports   123

12   Recurring entries   135

13   Amending company details and managing data   139

14   Creating a password to protect data   143

Practice assessment questions   147

Practice assessment answers   167

Index   I.1

INTRODUCTION

HOW TO USE THESE MATERIALS

These Kaplan Publishing learning materials have been carefully designed to make your learning experience as easy as possible and to give you the best chance of success in your AAT assessments.

They contain a number of features to help you in the study process.

The sections on the Unit Guide, the Assessment and Study Skills should be read before you commence your studies.

They are designed to familiarise you with the nature and content of the assessment and to give you tips on how best to approach your studies.

STUDY TEXT

This study text has been specially prepared for the AQ2016 qualification introduced in September 2016.

It uses a case study approach to guide you through the syllabus and builds up your knowledge and skills chapter by chapter. The text is based upon Sage Business Cloud Accounting.

Quality and accuracy are of the utmost importance to us so if you spot an error in any of our products, please send an email to mykaplanreporting@kaplan.com with full details, or follow the link to the feedback form in MyKaplan.

Our Quality Co-ordinator will work with our technical team to verify the error and take action to ensure it is corrected in future editions.

UNIT GUIDE

INTRODUCTION

This unit provides students with the knowledge and skills needed to carry out typical bookkeeping transactions and tasks using accounting software. In the modern business environment, processing data and information into accounting software is a necessary task in most finance roles. This unit teaches students the practical steps for processing accounting information electronically and will allow students to reinforce their understanding of the sequence in which bookkeeping tasks are carried out.

On completion of this unit, students will have the practical ability to enter accounting transactions into accounting software and to perform bank reconciliations accurately. Students will be able to enter information into accounting software and understand the main features of accounting software. They will learn how to set up general ledger accounts for new and existing businesses and process the typical bookkeeping entries expected of students at this level, including the processing of sales and purchase documentation, recording bank and cash entries and carrying out bank reconciliations accurately. Students will also learn how to produce reports using the software and understand the purpose of these reports.

Students must have access to a suitable specialised accounting software package as part of their study for this unit and for the assessment. Spreadsheet software alone will not allow full unit content coverage, so cannot be used for the study or assessment of this unit. The program selected by learning providers must be capable of producing reports in at least one of the following formats at various stages of the process: XLS, XLSX, CSV, DOC, DOCX, PDF, BMP, GIF, JPEG, PNG.

Screenshots may also be submitted using one of these formats. Assessment evidence submitted in alternative file formats will not be marked.

Using Accounting Software is a **mandatory** unit in this qualification.

Learning objectives

On completion of these units the learner will be able to:

- Set up accounting software

- Process sales and purchases transactions

- Process bank and cash transactions

- Perform period end routine tasks

- Produce reports

Scope of content

The specific items contained within each learning outcome and where to find them in this study text are detailed below.

Chapter

Set up accounting software

1.1	**Enter information relating to organisation at the beginning of an accounting period**	7
	• set up and amend the general ledger accounts	
	• enter the relevant opening balance information	
1.2	**Set up customer accounts**	6
	• create customer accounts	
	• enter the relevant opening balance information	
1.3	**Set up supplier accounts**	5
	• create supplier accounts	
	• enter the relevant opening balance information	

Chapter

Process sales and purchases transactions

| 2.1 | **Process sales invoices and credit notes** | 8 |

- process sales invoices from source documents ensuring VAT (where applicable) is posted to the correct account

- process credit notes from source documents ensuring VAT (where applicable) is posted to the correct account

| 2.2 | **Allocate receipts from customers** | 8 |

- process receipts from customers and allocate amounts correctly: in full payment, in part payment, against the opening balance, invoices and credit notes

| 2.3 | **Process purchase invoices and credit notes** | 8 |

- process purchase invoices and source documents ensuring VAT (where applicable) is posted to the correct account

- process credit notes from source documents ensuring VAT (where applicable) is posted to the correct account

| 2.4 | **Allocate payments to suppliers** | 8 |

- process payments to suppliers and allocate amounts correctly: in full payment, in part payment, against the opening balance, invoices and credit notes

Process bank and cash transactions

| 3.1 | **Process receipts and payments for non-credit transactions** | 8 |

- process bank and cash receipts ensuring VAT (where applicable) is posted to the correct account

- process bank and cash payments ensuring VAT (where applicable) is posted to the correct account

		Chapter
3.2	**Process recurring receipts and payments**	12

- set up and process a recurring bank receipt
- set up and process a recurring bank payment

| **3.3** | **Process petty cash receipts and payments** | 8 |

- how to top up petty cash
- process petty cash payments ensuring VAT (where applicable) is posted to the correct account
- process petty cash receipts ensuring VAT (where applicable) is posted to the correct account

Perform period end routine tasks

| **4.1** | **Process journals** | 9 |

- process journals: to correct errors, to record unrecorded transactions or adjustments

| **4.2** | **Reconcile the bank statement** | 10 |

- how to agree the payments and receipts for the period from the bank statement to the bank entries made on accounting software
- process unrecorded payments and receipts
- reconcile the bank balance at the end of an accounting period

Produce reports

| **5.1** | **Produce routine reports for customers and suppliers** | 5, 6, 8, 11 |

- how to identify the customer or supplier report required
- produce reports that meet business requirements

		Chapter
5.2	**Produce routine reports from the general ledger**	4, 7, 8, 9, 10, 11

- produce a trial balance and audit trail

- identify additional general ledger reports required

- produce reports that meet business requirements

Delivering this unit

Unit name	Content links	Suggested order of delivery
Bookkeeping Transactions	Manual bookkeeping skills are useful underpinning knowledge for Using Accounting Software.	It is recommended that Bookkeeping Transactions is delivered either before or at the same time as this unit.
Bookkeeping Controls	Control account reconciliations and basic journal adjustments offer useful underpinning knowledge for Using Accounting Software.	It is recommended that Bookkeeping Controls is delivered either before or at the same time as this unit.

KAPLAN PUBLISHING

THE ASSESSMENT

Test specification for this unit assessment

Assessment type	Marking type	Duration of exam
Computer based unit assessment	Human marked	2 hours

Learning outcomes		Weighting
1	Set up accounting software	25%
2	Process sales and purchases transactions	35%
3	Process bank and cash transactions	20%
4	Perform period end routine tasks	15%
5	Produce reports	5%
Total		**100%**

STUDY SKILLS

Preparing to study

Devise a study plan

Determine which times of the week you will study.

Split these times into sessions of at least one hour for study of new material. Any shorter periods could be used for revision or practice.

Put the times you plan to study onto a study plan for the weeks from now until the assessment and set yourself targets for each period of study – in your sessions make sure you cover the whole course, activities and the associated questions in the workbook at the back of the manual.

If you are studying more than one unit at a time, try to vary your subjects as this can help to keep you interested and see subjects as part of wider knowledge.

When working through your course, compare your progress with your plan and, if necessary, re-plan your work (perhaps including extra sessions) or, if you are ahead, do some extra revision/practice questions.

Effective studying

Active reading

You are not expected to learn the text by rote, rather, you must understand what you are reading and be able to use it to pass the assessment and develop good practice.

A good technique is to use SQ3Rs – Survey, Question, Read, Recall, Review:

1 **Survey the chapter**

   Look at the headings and read the introduction, knowledge, skills and content, so as to get an overview of what the chapter deals with.

2 **Question**

   Whilst undertaking the survey ask yourself the questions you hope the chapter will answer for you.

3   Read

Read through the chapter thoroughly working through the activities and, at the end, making sure that you can meet the learning objectives highlighted on the first page.

4   Recall

At the end of each section and at the end of the chapter, try to recall the main ideas of the section/chapter without referring to the text. This is best done after a short break of a couple of minutes after the reading stage.

5   Review

Check that your recall notes are correct.

You may also find it helpful to re-read the chapter to try and see the topic(s) it deals with as a whole.

Note taking

Taking notes is a useful way of learning, but do not simply copy out the text.

The notes must:

- be in your own words
- be concise
- cover the key points
- well organised
- be modified as you study further chapters in this text or in related ones.

Trying to summarise a chapter without referring to the text can be a useful way of determining which areas you know and which you don't.

Three ways of taking notes

1   Summarise the key points of a chapter

2   Make linear notes

A list of headings, subdivided with sub-headings listing the key points.

If you use linear notes, you can use different colours to highlight key points and keep topic areas together.

Use plenty of space to make your notes easy to use.

3   Try a diagrammatic form

The most common of which is a mind map.

To make a mind map, put the main heading in the centre of the paper and put a circle around it.

Draw lines radiating from this to the main sub-headings which again have circles around them.

Continue the process from the sub-headings to sub-sub-headings.

Annotating the text

You may find it useful to underline or highlight key points in your study text – but do be selective.

You may also wish to make notes in the margins.

Revision phase

Kaplan has produced material specifically designed for your final assessment preparation for this unit.

Further guidance on how to approach the final stage of your studies is given in these materials.

Further reading

In addition to this text, you should also read the 'Accounting Technician' magazine every month to keep abreast of any guidance from the examiners.

An introduction to computerised accounting

1

Introduction

The aim of this manual is to guide you through the computerised accounting aspects of your studies.

To complete this manual you will need an understanding of the basics of double entry bookkeeping and you will need to be signed up to Sage Business Cloud Accounting **(formerly Sage One)** which is an online integrated computerised software system for accounting. Sage recently re-branded the product from Sage One to Sage Business Cloud Accounting.

If you have another version of SAGE, or even another accounting package, you may not be able to use this manual efficiently.

Instructions for signing up to Sage Business Cloud Accounting are provided in the next chapter.

Sage Business Cloud Accounting is an online service, and will be updated on a regular basis (every 2 or 3 weeks) some updates will include minor improvements and additional features, others will be much more significant. When updates are made you will be notified with a message accessed directly from Sage Business Cloud Accounting. Students are advised to read these messages and understand them. The printed copy of this text is based on the Sage Business Cloud Accounting service at the point of publishing and therefore some of the screens and navigation that you see may have changed slightly.

This text uses a **case study approach** to guide you step-by-step. It assumes that you have never used a computerised accounting system before. Even if you have, it is worth starting at the beginning to ensure that you don't 'jump ahead' too quickly.

ASSESSMENT CRITERIA

An introduction to using accounting software

CONTENTS

1 Manual and computerised bookkeeping

2 Benefits of a computerised system

3 Accounting documents

4 Coding

5 Risks of using a computerised system

KAPLAN PUBLISHING

1 Manual and computerised bookkeeping

The double entry system of bookkeeping that is still used today was developed in Italy in the fifteenth century. With the introduction of affordable and reliable information technology in the last thirty years, it was perhaps inevitable that business organisations would look to find ways to computerise their bookkeeping systems. Now it is rare to find an organisation which does not use some form of computer to aid the day-to-day record keeping that is an essential part of running a business whether large or small.

For very small organisations, a simple spreadsheet to record monies in and out of the business may suffice. However, once a business becomes larger or more complex, it may be beneficial to introduce a computerised bookkeeping system. There are many proprietary versions on the market, each of which works in a similar way. However, they will each offer different approaches to data entry, presentation of reports and so on, as well as different 'extras' such as stock management modules, budgeting and tax planning. Some systems, including Sage Business Cloud Accounting, also allow a business to integrate a computerised payroll function.

2 Benefits of a computerised system

The main benefits of a computerised bookkeeping system are:

- quicker, more efficient processing of data

- fewer mathematical errors – because the system completes all the double entry and other mathematical functions (e.g. calculation of percentages) there is reduced opportunity for human error

- accounting documents (e.g. invoices, statements etc.) can be generated automatically, using tailored documents designed to incorporate company details, logos etc.

- the range of information that can be easily produced in reports is wide and varied, meaning businesses can report to various internal and external groups (e.g. management, directors, shareholders, banks etc.) in an appropriate format

- there is no need for manual processing of data – computerised bookkeeping systems complete all the double entry automatically

- hardware and software prices have fallen dramatically over the last thirty years, making a computerised system affordable to all organisations

- allow data to be easily transferred into other programs – e.g. a spreadsheet or word processing package.

3 Accounting documents

Business organisations rely on relevant documentation to record the transactions that it undertakes. Without an appropriate piece of supporting documentation, there is no way of knowing what has been bought, from whom and for how much, nor indeed what has been sold. With a high proportion of modern transactions being on credit, an accurate and comprehensive system of recording transactions is essential.

Many business documents are referred to as '**Primary Records**'. They include:

- purchase orders

- delivery notes

- purchase invoices

- credit notes

- sales invoices.

These documents are used to record business transactions in the first instance. For example, if an organisation wishes to purchase a new computer printer, it may first raise a **purchase order** which is sent to the supplier. The supplier would issue or deliver the printer along with a **delivery note**, to record the safe receipt of the goods. A **supplier invoice** requiring payment would follow. If the printer was faulty, it could be returned and a **credit note** issued.

In order for a transaction to be correctly recorded in a computerised accounting system, the appropriate documentation must first be raised and then the details entered into 'the system'; indeed, many organisations employ accounting staff whose job is primarily to enter the data accurately and completely from the source documents.

There are many other documents which are also essential in maintaining an up-to-date and accurate accounting system. Bank statements, schedules of direct debits/standing orders, supplier statements, correspondence from suppliers and customers and so on also provide invaluable information which can be used to check the computerised bookkeeping system for accuracy.

In the course of the case study which follows, you will be required to enter details from a range of source documents and use other documents to maintain a computerised bookkeeping system for a small company.

4 Coding

All computerised bookkeeping systems work by the use of codes. Each supplier and each customer must be given a unique code by which the computer software can recognise them. It is vital that there can be no confusion between two suppliers with similar names. For example, you may be fully aware that John Green and John Greenwood are entirely different people, but it could be easy for a computer to mix them up. Each must therefore be given a unique code by which they can be identified.

Similarly, each product manufactured or sold by an organisation may be given a unique code. Also, employees are usually 'coded' – you could check your pay slip to find your own Employee Reference Number.

Finally, every type of income or expense, asset or liability, is given a unique code to identify it. This makes entering transactions quite straightforward, since you need only refer to the relevant four digit code rather than a long narrative description.

Codes must be unique. However, they should also be recognisable by the person dealing with the system. For example, if a supplier was coded "SMITH006", this would be far more recognisable than a purely numeric code such as "0827329".

Care must be taken to issue codes that are not ambiguous. The use of a combination of letters and numbers (an alphanumeric code) often achieves this.

In Sage Business Cloud Accounting, when you create a new customer or supplier record, you are provided with a 10 character limited alpha-numeric field to enter the customer or supplier code. The code can be whatever you require the code to be as long as it is unique within the system and 10 characters or less. Many organisations have a set structure for coding, and if this is the case in your organisation you should follow it.

5 Risks of using a computerised system

Computerised accounting systems may offer a lot of advantages to businesses, but organisations must also be aware of the potential risks posed by such systems. These risks can be categorised as:

- **Physical risks** – caused by system failure, theft, damage or loss or corruption of data and of access to systems or data by unauthorised users (e.g. by a compromise to password security)

- **Virus threats** – the risk of a computer virus (or similar) being introduced to a network, with the resultant loss of or damage to data

- **Legal threats** – from contravention of legislation such as the Data Protection Act (1998) by an organisation in the way that it stores or uses personal data.

Accounting data is particularly at risk, because it is highly confidential and potentially highly valuable to other people. Hence you must remain especially vigilant to risks to data security.

Virus threats

All computers that are linked to 'the outside world' (e.g. via a network or to the internet) are susceptible to security threats. Many people are familiar with the threat posed by viruses or other similar threats.

A virus is a piece of software that is used to maliciously infect your computer. What is more, it then has the ability to replicate itself and infect any other computer that is connected to yours. Of course, this also means that your computer is at risk of being infected by other computers as well.

Introduction of the virus to a system usually takes place when you open a file that has been deliberately infected – for example, an email attachment or a web-site, an infected piece of software, or an infected memory device (e.g. a memory stick).

The consequences of being infected by a virus are many:

- infecting all other computers you are linked to

- deleting particular files – especially files which are essential to the normal operation of your computer

- altering files so they are no longer legible

- slowing down your computer by taking up huge amounts of memory – leaving your computer extremely slow and unable to perform basic tasks

- accessing your data and sending it to other people

- 'reading' your passwords for essential sites such as on-line banking – enabling somebody else to access your bank account

- wiping your hard-drive – deleting everything from the computer.

Safeguards against viruses

Firewalls: these are designed to prevent hackers gaining access to a computer network via the phone line. These can be a piece of software (now often built in to operating systems such as Windows) or a hardware firewall, which is effectively a box which acts as a barrier between the modem (the phone line into your computer) and the computer itself. An effective firewall is an essential aspect of computer safeguarding, particularly where users have access to the internet.

Effective IT policies: most organisations now have clearly defined IT policies regarding the private use of the internet and e-mails, not allowing employees to install their own software (e.g. games) on work computers.

Using virus protection software: this is the most important method of protecting computer systems. It acts as a guard dog, constantly watching for suspicious files, blocking or destroying them and advising the user that there has been an attempt to compromise the security of the system. As virus protection programs are constantly being updated with details of new viruses, it is essential that it is kept updated and current at all times. An out-of-date program is no protection against the most recent viruses.

Personal vigilance: Be very wary if you receive unsolicited emails from addresses that you do not recognise. Do not open any emails that you are suspicious of – you should report these to your IT manager or your supervisor. However, you should also be wary of emails (particularly those with attachments) from addresses you **do** recognise – remember, if somebody you know has a computer which has been infected there is a high probability that their computer will then try to attack your computer as well.

Be very careful when accessing the internet. Only use sites you need for work. Be wary of links to other sites that you do not recognise. Again, if you are in any doubt, or suspect that your computer may have fallen victim to a virus, inform your supervisor.

Passwords

Passwords are one of the most common – and most abused – forms of computer security. In most businesses the access to each computer is protected by a password, as well as access to different pieces of software. Even individual files and documents can and should be protected if they contain confidential or sensitive information.

The choice of password is very important; you should be able to remember it, but it should not be easily guessed by others. Ideally, a password should:

- be at least 6–8 characters long
- contain a mixture of upper and lower case letters, numbers and symbols
- not be a recognisable word.

Under no circumstances should you choose something like your own name, your child's name or your pet dog's name – these are far too easy for someone with only a small amount of knowledge about you to guess. You should also avoid obvious combinations such as 'password' or '123456'.

You should be able to remember your own password. Do not be tempted to write it down in your diary, on a scrap of paper in your top drawer, or on a sticky note attached to the monitor!

You should also never tell anybody else your password – even your most trusted colleague. If you do suspect that somebody knows what your password is you should change it immediately.

Many systems are configured to require you to change your password every few weeks – even if yours is not, this is good practice.

Backups

Sage Business Cloud Accounting is a cloud based computer system and as such does not require the end user to perform backups. Backups are automatic and are managed by Sage.

Since the AAT Exam and syllabus is generic and not aligned to any one particular accounting system, internet based or otherwise, you can for the purposes of the exam (if required) show how you would export the audit trial report as a form of backup. How to do this will be covered in a later Chapter.

Signing up to Sage Business Cloud Accounting

CONTENTS

There are no relevant 'learning outcomes' applicable to this section of the workbook, as you will not be required to sign up to Sage Business Cloud Accounting **(formerly Sage One)** as part of the AAT assessment. Therefore, this particular chapter is designed to assist you with the initial set up process that will enable you to start using Sage Business Cloud Accounting for the first time as part of your UACS studies.

1 Signing up to Sage Business Cloud Accounting

Signing up to Sage Business Cloud Accounting **(formerly Sage One)** for use on your UACS course is very straightforward.

(1)   Log in to your MyKaplan account:

http://mykaplan.co.uk

Click in to your UACS course line then from the table of contents select 'SageOne Access' then SageOne Registration

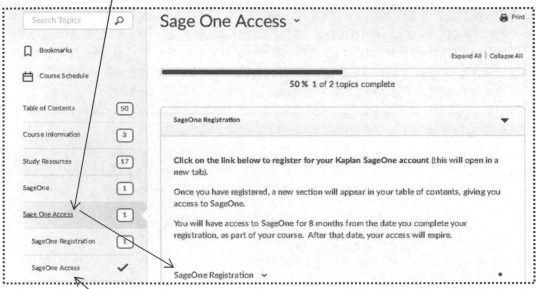

(2)   Each time you wish to access your account once you have registered, you need to log in to your MyKaplan account. Go to the table of contents and select 'Sage One Access' and you will be taken back in to your Sage Business Cloud Accounting account.

Setting up your company

3

CONTENTS

1 Case Study – background to the company

2 Setting up the company

As with the previous chapter, there are no 'learning outcomes' associated with this chapter of the workbook.

During the AAT UACS assessment, you will be required to enter information to match the details of the company given in the scenario within the real assessment. This will include the name and address of the company and also the details of their financial year.

1 Case Study – background to the company

You will be given a case study throughout this workbook which will form the basis for activities for you to practise on Sage Business Cloud Accounting. It relates to a fictitious company called **TotalPhoto**. By completing the activities and entering the relevant transactions, you will learn how to do lots of tasks that are available on Sage Business Cloud Accounting. You will also help prepare for the AAT UACS computer based assessment as part of your AAT studies.

Background to TotalPhoto

TotalPhoto is a small company based in the market town of Miltonby, in Lancashire. It is owned by two directors, Matt Evans and Stuart Lincoln. It was established in 2004 when both Matt and Stuart left Art College. They specialise in contemporary family photography, most of which takes place in their rented studio on a small industrial estate on the outskirts of town. In addition, they also undertake a varied and increasing range of contracted photography, including weddings, dance shows, football competitions etc.

TotalPhoto has four members of staff, excluding yourself. In addition to Matt and Stuart, there is Sarala, a part-time photographer, and Michelle, the administrator for the company.

Since its inception, the company has used a manual bookkeeping system. However, the company has grown significantly in this time and Matt and Stuart now require more timely financial information with which to manage the company. They have therefore decided to implement a computerised system and to employ you as a part-time bookkeeper for the business.

The first day of the company's financial year is 1st October 20XX. You may use any year but do ensure that all transactions fall within the relevant dates.

2 Setting up the company

Introduction

When you start using Sage Business Cloud Accounting for your case study company, you must first enter some information about the company itself. This is important because it will identify this particular company and appear on various reports. In addition, at this stage, you must enter the dates of the company's financial year.

When you click to sign up to Sage Business Cloud Accounting from your MyKaplan account, the business name will automatically default to **'Kaplan Financial'.** You are unable to change this name but could add the scenario name you are working on, into the first line of the address if you wish. The first case study in this book is 'TotalPhoto'.

Data

You will need the following information for this session.

Company Name:	TotalPhoto
Company Address:	Unit 63 Bailey Industrial Estate Fornby Road Miltonby Lancashire LD37 7QZ
Telephone:	01949 969 378
Fax:	01949 969 379
E-mail:	info@totalphoto.webnet.uk
Website:	www.totalphoto.co.uk
Company Reg. Number:	734928107
VAT Number:	376 096 823
Accounting Period:	1st October 20XX – 30th September 20XX

Now we can begin entering the data for our company, TotalPhoto.

Activity

Enter the information onto the computerised system using the information provided in the previous box. Guidance follows.

When you access your Sage Business Cloud Accounting account for the first time you will notice a series of set up options.

STEP ONE Type of company – Select the 'Sole Trader or Small Business' for the type of company. Save and continue.

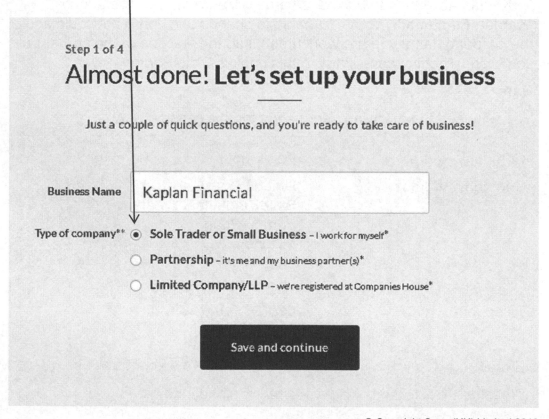

Step 1 of 4

Almost done! Let's set up your business

Just a couple of quick questions, and you're ready to take care of business!

Business Name | Kaplan Financial

Type of company** ● **Sole Trader or Small Business** – I work for myself*

○ **Partnership** – it's me and my business partner(s)*

○ **Limited Company/LLP** – we're registered at Companies House*

Save and continue

STEP TWO Addresses – Enter the company address and telephone number. Save and continue. (You could also add 'TotalPhoto in the first line of the address, this is optional)

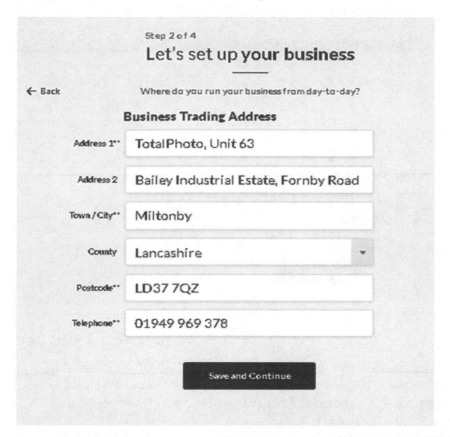

Step 2 of 4

Let's set up your business

← Back

Where do you run your business from day-to-day?

Business Trading Address

Address 1** | TotalPhoto, Unit 63

Address 2 | Bailey Industrial Estate, Fornby Road

Town / City** | Miltonby

County | Lancashire

Postcode** | LD37 7QZ

Telephone** | 01949 969 378

Save and Continue

STEP THREE Registered/VAT – Select standard and enter the VAT Number in the field. Click 'All done!'.

Be sure to check for accuracy when entering transactions in Sage Business Cloud Accounting – but don't worry if you make a mistake because you can always amend it later (we will look at how you can amend errors in a later chapter).

You will now be returned to the main Getting Started Area.

If the message below appears you can click on the small cross in the top right corner. These settings are not currently a requirement for your studies.

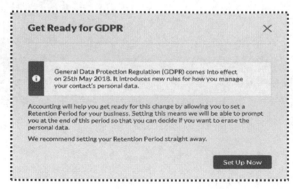

FINANCIAL SETTINGS – Select 'Settings' on the top row, then 'Accounting Dates & VAT'.

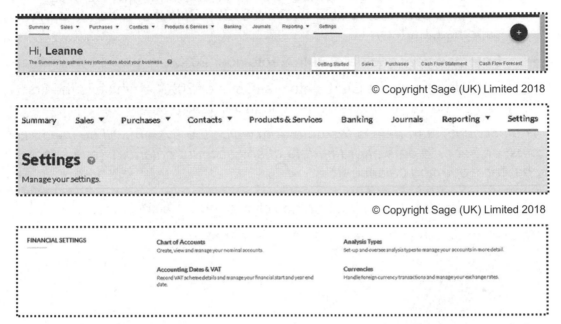

Enter your financial settings

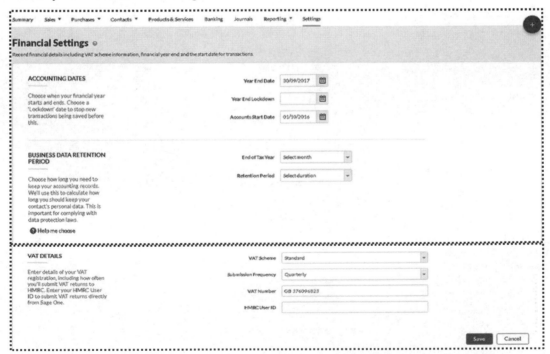

This is a really important stage. You need to enter the dates of your company's Financial Year and their VAT details. Remember, for TotalPhoto the company's Financial Year is 1st October 20XX to 30th September 20XX. You can ignore the Business Data Retention.

Period fields.

- The VAT Registration Number should be showing from the initial set-up screen (the number is 376096823). Select the Standard VAT scheme/Quarterly.

- Enter the year end date: 30th September 20XX.

- Enter the Accounts Start Date: 1st October 20XX – which is the first day of the TotalPhoto's current financial year.

The accounts start date is the date from which the system will be used. It must be set on a date after the date of any account balances (see later chapter – opening balances)

Once you are happy with your entries click on the [Save] button.

You will be taken to the Settings Overview area.

Navigating Sage Business Cloud Accounting

Introduction

You have by now created your Sage Business Cloud Accounting and set up the basic details of the company. The next stage is to practice navigating your way around the different sections of Sage Business Cloud Accounting. Don't worry if you have never used a package like this before, it is very user-friendly and with lots of practice you will become comfortable with the different functions and areas covered.

ASSESSMENT CRITERIA
Navigating Sage Business Cloud Accounting
Produce routine reports from the general ledger (5.2)

CONTENTS	
1	Menus and functions
2	Entering new data and editing or correcting existing data
3	Running reports
4	Backing up your work

1 Menus and functions

Sage Business Cloud Accounting is a web browser based system and can be securely accessed from any computer connected to the internet that is equipped with internet browser software. Microsoft Explorer, Safari and Google Chrome are examples of the browsers that can be used to access Sage Business Cloud Accounting. It is recommended that you use the latest, most up to date, version of the browser that you choose e.g. Internet explorer, Safari or Chrome.

Sage Business Cloud Accounting will operate inside a single browser tab or, if required, multiple browser tabs.

When you login to Sage Business Cloud Accounting you will be directed to the Summary area. The specific tab within the summary area you will first see will depend on which one you last used when you logged out previously.

Black Navigation Bar and Feedback Tab

The black bar menu at the very top of the Sage Business Cloud Accounting is used to navigate between businesses if you have more than one and also between systems. It also contains links to your account area and message centre. In addition you can access settings and help guides and logout from here.

Changing businesses and systems will not be required for UACS. Student subscriptions of Sage Business Cloud Accounting are supplied as Single company versions, you should not attempt to add additional companies to your subscription.

When we look at reporting, the black bar is also used to navigate to saved reports.

© Copyright Sage (UK) Limited 2018

The Feedback tab allows you to send a message directly to Sage to let them know what you feel about the service.

THIS IS NOT TO BE USED TO ACCESS SUPPORT OR ASK QUESTIONS.

Top menu

Sage Business Cloud Accounting features are grouped by functional area using the menu options as shown above. By hovering over each menu item you are able to view and select from the items available. To select just click the item you want, this includes the top item which is permanently displayed.

Summary screens

By selecting Summary from the top menu you will then be able to navigate to summary dashboard information about each functional area. The summary area also includes the Getting Started information described earlier.

The summary screens will initially not show any data and graphs and charts will be empty. As we go through this course and enter transactions feel free to pop back to this area and have a look at how the data that you have entered has been represented.

The summary area is used by business people, bookkeepers and accountants to get quick insights into the performance of the business and understand any problems regarding debts and cash flow (for example).

Grids, filters and toolbar functions

Having selected an item from one of the top menus (e.g. Sales/Quick Entries) a grid will appear listing either transactions or other things, such as contacts or products depending what has been chosen. The list content will depend on what you have chosen, based on dates.

© Copyright Sage (UK) Limited 2018

You can search the grid using the search field using reference numbers, names etc.

The column entries will appear and enable you to select which ones you require. As we haven't entered any data yet, please see an example below:

Grid tool bar

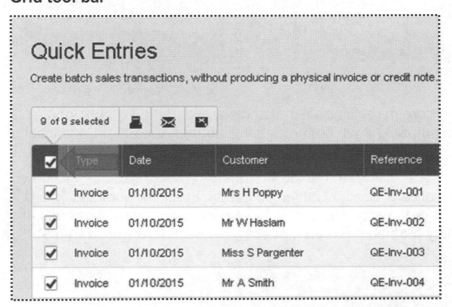

© Copyright Sage (UK) Limited 2018

As you select all of the items in the grid (add a tick on the top left box), or individual items, the grid toolbar will appear, allowing you to perform actions on the items you have selected (as indicated by the ticks). The toolbar will allow you to perform a number of actions depending on the content of the grid including; printing to pdf/csv and emailing of the list.

There are lots of different grid views and types throughout Sage Business Cloud Accounting, but they are all operated more or less the same way. The differences will become more apparent as you get used to using the system.

`Date ↑` In addition, the grid of data can be sorted by column headings. Click on the heading you wish to sort by and sort ascending or descending.

Online context help

Throughout Sage Business Cloud Accounting you will notice the ❓ symbol. This will allow you to access the online help system. The help page you are taken to will depend on where you were in the system when it was selected. This means you usually get the page you are looking for straight away.

From the black navigation bar, by selecting `Help` here you will be taken to the Sage Business Cloud Accounting help centre. Using the menus and search functions contained here, you will be able to locate help content you require.

This can also be accessed using the following URL if you are not logged into Sage Business Cloud Accounting. https://help.sageone.com/en_uk/accounting/index.html. This is a great source of information and can be used alongside this text.

Drill-down enquiry

Throughout Sage Business Cloud Accounting it is generally possible to click on a transaction or data item listed in a grid or a report and drill down to the next level or to a source entry. This applies to the grids described in this chapter.

2 Entering new data and editing or correcting existing data

New data

Entering transactions or other items such as customers and suppliers will be covered in detail in a later chapter. To access the input screens for a new item or transaction use the blue action buttons.

Here are some examples:

The multi-action button will allow you to perform multiple actions. As well as creating new transactions or records you will be able to use these buttons to access the import features when data is available outside of Sage Business Cloud Accounting or to create other related transaction types.

You will not be required to import data as part of UACS.

Editing and correcting data

Once a transaction such as an invoice or a bank item is entered into Sage Business Cloud Accounting it can be viewed at any time. Accounting transactions appear in reports grids and if you need to look at the item you can 'click' on it and it will open in a screen very similar to the one which was used to create it.

In addition to viewing previously entered items or records it is also possible to edit them i.e. adding/deleting information. Some accounting transactions will have limitations on what can be edited depending on their status. Invoices allocated to a payment for example or banking items reconciled in the bank reconciliation module will become fully or partly locked depending on the transaction type.

There are other ways to correct accounting information if the transaction itself cannot be changed. One way is to use a journal, which will be covered in a later chapter.

3 Running reports

Reports will be covered separately in a later chapter, in terms of their content and meaning, however to access the Sage Business Cloud Accounting standard reports; select the 'Reporting' option from the main screen and you will be presented with a series of reports to choose from.

These reports are pre-configured in terms of their data fields (columns) and format, style and layout.

To select the content or the data you require for the given report use the period field i.e. this month or custom and select your chosen dates then click calculate. This will also enable you to access the selection criteria and filter options such as dates, statuses, transaction types and analysis groups etc.

© Copyright Sage (UK) Limited 2018

4 Backing up your work

It is important to guard against accidental losses which can prove very costly and time-consuming to recover or re-input. Being confident that your data is being saved regularly is critical and keeping a backup of your data should become part of your daily routine.

As we saw earlier, Sage Business Cloud Accounting is an internet based computer system and does not require the end user to perform backups. Backups are automatic and are managed by Sage.

However, if you did you need to show how you would export the audit trial report as a form of backup. Work through the following screens to learn how to do this.

Reporting drop down menu, select 'More':

From the reporting menu, select Audit Trail:

KAPLAN PUBLISHING

Using the 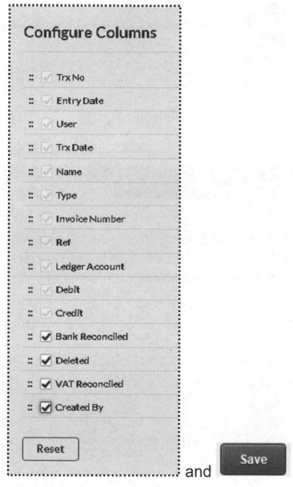 column configurator add/remove the columns of data you would like to display:

Configure Columns

:: ☑ Trx No

:: ☑ Entry Date

:: ☑ User

:: ☑ Trx Date

:: ☑ Name

:: ☑ Type

:: ☑ Invoice Number

:: ☑ Ref

:: ☑ Ledger Account

:: ☑ Debit

:: ☑ Credit

:: ☑ Bank Reconciled

:: ☑ Deleted

:: ☑ VAT Reconciled

:: ☑ Created By

Reset

and Save

Using the Period Custom Period function, select custom and reporting dates as required for all transaction types. You must select 'Calculate' to then view the relevant requested data onscreen. As you will learn later in this book, any opening balances will default to the last day of the previous financial year so will always need including when producing most of the Sage Business Cloud Accounting reports.

Audit Trail Breakdown
The audit trail breakdown is a detailed record of all transactions posted. You can view this by transaction type for a specified date range.

Period Custom | From 30/09/2016 | To 30/09/2017 | More | Calculate | Summary | Export

Using the Export function, you can select CSV

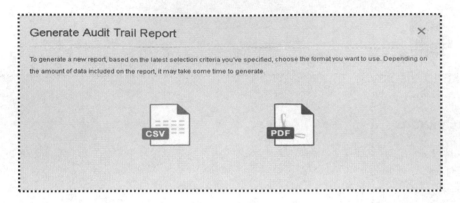

The report will run and to access the report go to the black bar as shown:

Select Open and Save. The file will download and the audit trail report will display in Excel. This is a demonstration and you can follow these steps later. You will not have any data to include in the report at this stage.

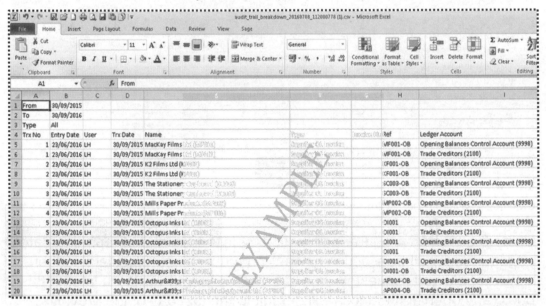

Setting up your suppliers' details

5

Introduction

Most business organisations will, over time, deal with a wide range of suppliers. For example, a café may have different suppliers for their meat, cheese, vegetables, wine etc. A hairdresser will buy different products from different suppliers. Sometimes supplies will be obtained from a wholesaler or a cash and carry; other supplies may be sourced directly from the manufacturers.

The organisation will need to keep very accurate and timely records of all transactions with their suppliers. These transactions will typically include:

(1) purchases and returns

(2) discounts received from the supplier

(3) payments made to the supplier by cash, cheque or bank transfer in settlement of outstanding bills.

In addition, it would be very convenient to have all the contact details of every supplier easily to hand.

Fortunately Sage Business Cloud Accounting provides a comprehensive supplier management system which covers all these requirements. You will see how this works shortly, but firstly you will need to enter your suppliers' details.

ASSESSMENT CRITERIA	CONTENTS	
Set up supplier accounts (1.3)	1	Supplier data
Produce routine reports for customers and suppliers (5.1)	2	Entering supplier details
	3	Printing supplier data reports
	4	Supplier opening balances

1 Supplier data

We can now start inputting some data on to the computerised system using our case study firm, TotalPhoto.

 Activity

TotalPhoto has six suppliers whose details are given below. Enter these onto the computerised system. Guidance on how to enter these records for suppliers follows.

Supplier details

Mackay Films Ltd	**A/c Ref: MF001**

33 West Parade
Miltonby
Lancashire
LN87 7HD

Tel 01828 827493

Contact: Carl Richardson

Outstanding Balance at 30th September 20XX: **£345.36**

Credit Terms: **30 days**

K2 Films Ltd	**A/c Ref: KF001**

Tokyo House
72-84 Great Milne Street
London
WC4 6DD

Tel 0207 867 6599

Contact: Kim Nakajima

Outstanding Balance at 30th September 20XX: **£1,726.55**

Credit Terms: **30 days**

The Stationery Cupboard　　　　　　　　　**A/c Ref: SC003**
21 Potter Way
Hull
Humberside
HU87 6YY

Tel 01482 417378

Contact: Alan Pensill

Outstanding Balance at 30th September 20XX: **£375.00**

Credit Terms: **14 days**

Mills Paper Products　　　　　　　　　**A/c Ref: MP002**
405 Ream Road
Bradford
West Yorkshire
BD5 6QA

Tel 01726 378918

Contact: Shaun Squire

Outstanding Balance at 30th September 20XX: **£4,920.30**

Credit Terms: **21 days**

Octopus Inks Ltd　　　　　　　　　**A/c Ref: OI001**
Unit 12
Longley Industrial Park
Gateshead
Tyne and Wear
GH77 5TG

Tel 0191 252 4132

Contact: Sheila Cribbley

Outstanding Balance at 30th September 20XX: **£550.20**

Credit Terms: **30 days**

Arthur's Photographic Equipment Ltd   **A/c Ref: AP004**
77 Overton Lane
Birmingham
BM97 8YK

Tel 0121 299 0192

Contact: Jennie Reeves

Outstanding Balance at 30th September 20XX: **£11,275.00**

Credit Terms: **30 days**

2 Entering supplier details

Supplier Set up

The first supplier to enter is:

Mackay Films Ltd
33 West Parade
Miltonby
Lancashire
LN87 7HD

Tel 01828 827493

Contact: Carl Richardson   **A/c Ref: MF001**

From the 'Contacts' menu, select the Suppliers option, you will be taken to the suppliers list.

The suppliers list will display all the suppliers which have previously been set up. By default these will be sorted in alphabetical order, however it is possible to re-sort the order by clicking on the column heading you wish to sort by.

KAPLAN PUBLISHING

It is possible to import suppliers from a data file, this is useful in a live work situation if you are moving from another accounting system and do not wish to enter all the supplier records manually into Sage Business Cloud Accounting. If you wish to experiment with this you can create a data file using Microsoft Excel by downloading the template which you can access from the help page.

To access the supplier set up use New Supplier button and the supplier set up page will open.

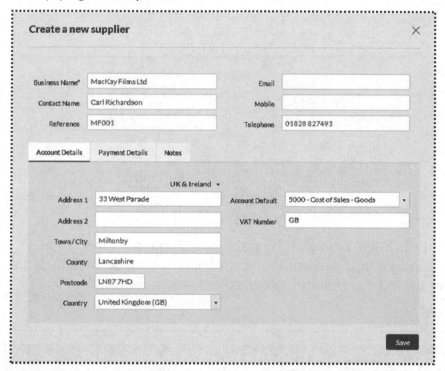

© Copyright Sage (UK) Limited 2018

Enter the business name in the Company/ Name field, the account reference.

If the supplier is VAT registered and you are aware of their VAT number this can be recorded here. Feel free to complete some sections with 'made up' information.

The Purchase Ledger (Nominal) Account will default to Cost of Sale Account 5000. This can be amended to the account you require but, for now, leave this unchanged.

Complete the contact information in the Account Details area as shown above.

Before you save the information you need to setup the Payment details:

Create a new supplier   ×

Business Name*	MacKay Films Ltd
Contact Name	Carl Richardson
Reference	MF001

Email	
Mobile	
Telephone	01828 827493

Account Details | **Payment Details** | Notes

PAYMENT TERMS   BANK DETAILS

☐ Set Credit Limit (£)	0.00	Account Name	
☑ Set Credit Terms	30 days	Sort Code	☐ . ☐ . ☐
		Account Number	
		BIC/Swift	
		IBAN	

Save

Place a tick in 'Set Credit Terms'. The default is 30 days. If the credit terms are not 30 days, you can amend accordingly. You may also in some situations have to add a credit limit which is just above.

Don't forget to SAVE!

Activity

You have already entered one of TotalPhoto's suppliers (Mackay Films Ltd).

You should now enter the full details for each of the remaining five suppliers, and then save them to Sage Business Cloud Accounting.

Once you have completed all 6 suppliers your supplier list will now be displaying 7 records including a record for HMRC.

To add or remove columns on this list, using the cog you will be able to select which columns are in view. In the example below the Email address has been removed and Credit Terms added.

The column order has remained unchanged, however to re-order columns click on the symbol ⠿ and drag the column to the required position.

3 Printing supplier data reports

Supplier data reports are available from the supplier list page.

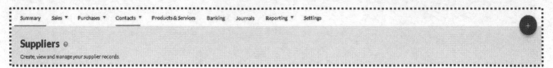

From the 'Contacts' menu, select the Suppliers option. You will be taken to the suppliers list.

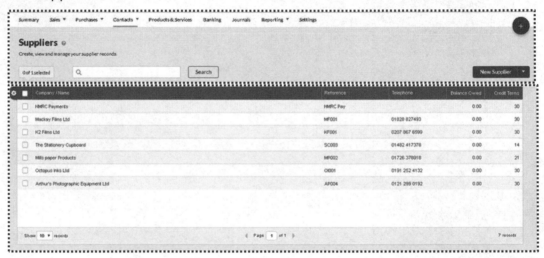

To access the reports you will need to select the suppliers which are required to be included in the report. This is done by selecting them in the list using the tick boxes to the left of the supplier name. To select all suppliers select the box at the top of the grid but then untick HMRC payments as we do not want to include those.

KAPLAN PUBLISHING

Having selected the suppliers you require, the supplier reports can be accessed.

Using the toolbar:

Select the printer icon 🖨 or pdf icon 📄 to send the supplier list to a printable report format:

TotalPhoto				
Company / Name	Reference	Telephone	Balance Owed	Credit Terms
Mackay Films Ltd	MF001	01828 827493	0.00	30
K2 Films Ltd	KF001	0207 867 6599	0.00	30
The Stationery Cupboard	SC003	01482 417378	0.00	14
Mills Paper Products	MP002	01726 378918	0.00	21
Octopus Inks Ltd	OI001	0191 252 4132	0.00	30
Arthur's Photographic Equipment Ltd	AP004	0121 299 0192	0.00	30

Using the More button _____ select Address List, to view the list of selected suppliers with their address details.

You will be asked which address types you require. You can select 'All' and then Generate.

Address List ✕

Select the address type(s) to display on this report

Address Types

All ▾

Generate   Cancel

To access the report, go to the black navigation bar reports icon to display available reports and click on the Supplier Address List option.

The report will appear showing all new suppliers.

	TotalPhoto					08 Jun 2017
	Supplier Address List					14:12

Address Types: All

Supplier Name	Address	Contact name	Phone	Mobile	Email	Fax
Mackay Films Ltd (MF001)	33 West Parade Miltonby Lancashire LN67 7HD	Carl Richardson	01828 827493			
K2 Films Ltd (KF001)	Tokyo House 72-84 Great Milne Street London WC4 6DD	Kim Nakajima	0207 867 6599			
The Stationery Cupboard (SC003)	21 Potter Way Hull Humberside HU87 6YY	Alan Pensill	01482 417378			
Mills Paper Products (MP002)	405 Ream Road Bradford West Yorkshire BD5 6QA	Shaun Squire	01726 378918			
Octopus Inks Ltd (OI001)	Unit 12 Longley Industrial Park Gateshead Tyne and Wear GH77 5TG	Sheila Cribbley	0191 252 4132			
Arthur's Photographic Equipment Ltd (AP004)	77 Overton Lane Birmingham BM97 8YK	Jennie Reeves	0121 299 0192			

4 Supplier opening balances

If you are operating a business and are transferring to a new accounting system, it is likely you will need to set the new system up with 'opening balances'. These include balances that are owed to suppliers.

A supplier balance is made up of all the invoices which are assigned to a supplier account which have either not be paid yet or matched/allocated with a payment on account. Occasionally invoices can be part-paid and the balance on the invoice is the unpaid part. Credit Notes and payments on account also need including as long as there is a balance outstanding on them.

In Sage Business Cloud Accounting it is possible to enter all the transactions making up the opening balance on an account or with a single sum total. Having the individual amounts is often better when managing a supplier account.

In the examples we are using, we have just a single opening balance for each supplier.

Supplier opening balances

The first supplier whose outstanding balance you should enter is:

Mackay Films Ltd
33 West Parade
Miltonby
Lancashire
LN87 7HD

Tel 01828 827493

Fax 01828 827493

Contact: Carl Richardson   **A/c Ref: MF001**

Outstanding Balance at 30th September 20XX: **£345.36**

To set up an opening balance go to the summary screen, then from the getting started tab, select the 'Enter money you to owe to suppliers' option.

Set up suppliers

1. Create or import suppliers ❷
2. Enter money you owe to suppliers ❷
3. Review the Aged Creditors report

After selection you will be taken to the Supplier Opening Balances page.

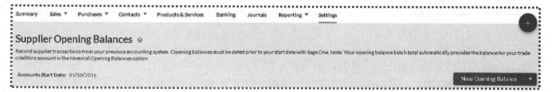

| Summary | Sales ▾ | Purchases ▾ | Contacts ▾ | Products & Services | Banking | Journals | Reporting ▾ | Settings |

Supplier Opening Balances ❷

Record supplier transactions from your previous accounting system. Opening balances must be dated prior to your start date with Sage One. Note: Your opening balance batch total automatically provides the balance for your trade creditors account in the Nominal Opening Balances option.

Accounts Start Date: 01/10/2016

New Opening Balance ▾

You will notice the 'Accounts Start Date' was set as 01/10/XX as the first day of the accounting period for the current year.

Select New Opening Balance [New Opening Balance ▾]. Using the screen provided enter the opening balance for Mackay Films as shown below.

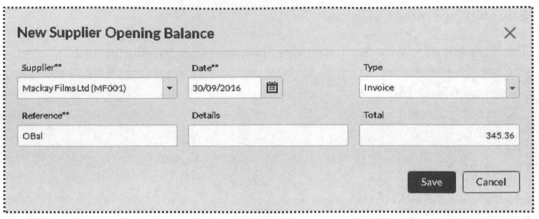

Use 'Invoice' as the type, the date defaults to 30th September 20XX, select Mackay Films Ltd. Opening Balances will always default to the last day of the **previous** financial year on Sage Business Cloud Accounting. This is acceptable and when producing reports later on, you can widen the date range to include opening balances. Since we are not entering information for a particular invoice, the reference and details should be something to help you identify this as a transaction. Then save.

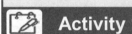 **Activity**

You have already entered one of TotalPhoto's suppliers opening balances (Mackay Films Ltd).

You should now enter the opening balance for each of the remaining five suppliers, and then save them to Sage Business Cloud Accounting.

Once you are complete your list of opening balances should look like this:

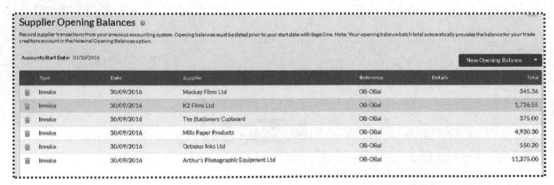

If you now return to the supplier list you will notice the opening balance now reflects in the balanced owed column.

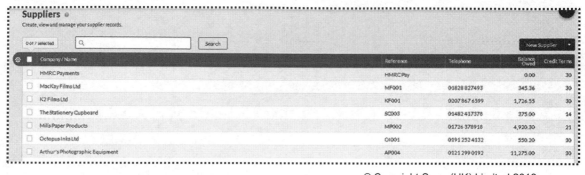

Setting up your customers' details

Introduction

Now that you have successfully entered your suppliers' details you can move on to enter relevant information about your customers as well.

The process of entering your customers' details is very similar to that of entering supplier information, so you should feel confident doing this now.

It is of course vitally important that you keep accurate records for each of your customers. This information is likely to include:

(1)   sales made on credit to customers, and sales returns

(2)   credit terms for your customers, including any discount they may receive

(3)   contact details for easy invoicing

(4)   payments received from customers.

Consistent, accurate recording of information is a vital aspect of any credit management system, ensuring that your organisation gets paid as quickly as possible for its sales. This can be the difference between failure and survival for most businesses.

LEARNING OBJECTIVES	CONTENTS	
Set up customer accounts (1.2)	1	Customer data
Produce routine reports for customers and suppliers (5.1)	2	Entering customer data
	3	Printing customer data reports

1 Customer data

We can now start to look at the 'Customers' process and begin with entering the initial information regarding our case study firm, TotalPhoto. Again, you will find detailed step by step instructions directly after this activity.

 Activity

TotalPhoto has six customers with outstanding balances as at 30th September 20XX. Their details and guidance on how to enter the customer details follow.

Mr W Haslam
22 Brown Street
Miltonby
Lancashire LN87 6FD
A/c Ref : HAS004

Amount outstanding at 30th September 20XX: £309.85

Credit terms: Payment in 14 days

Mrs H Poppy
120 Forrest Way
Miltonby
Lancashire LN87 9YR
A/c Ref : POP002

Amount outstanding at 30th September 20XX: £220.00

Credit terms: Payment in 14 days

Mrs T Pashby
30A Andrews Street
Killington
Lancashire LN85 6TT
A/c Ref: PAS002

Amount outstanding at 30th September 20XX: £89.50

Credit terms: Payment in 14 days

Campbell & Dunn Ltd
12 The Beeches
Miltonby
Lancashire LN87 9PP
A/c Ref: CAM004

Amount outstanding at 30th September 20XX: £2,056.85

Credit terms: Payment in 14 days

Lullabies Nursery
104 Victoria Road
Miltonby
Lancashire LN87 5PS
A/c Ref: LUL002

Amount outstanding at 30th September 20XX: £726.90

Credit terms: Payment in 14 days

Miss S Pargenter
11 Alexandra Park
Miltonby
Lancashire LN87 2WD
A/c Ref: PAR006

Amount outstanding at 30th September 20XX: £650.00

Credit terms: Payment in 14 days

You should now enter these six customers' details into Sage Business Cloud Accounting.

2 Entering customer data

Customer Set up

The first customer to enter is:

Mr W Haslam
22 Brown Street
Miltonby
Lancashire LN87 6FD
A/c Ref : HAS004

Amount outstanding at 30th September 20XX: £309.85

Credit terms: Payment in 14 days

From the 'Contacts' menu, select the Customers option. You will be taken to the Customer list.

The customers list will display all the customers which have previously been set up. By default these will be sorted in alphabetical order, however it is possible to re-sort the order by clicking on the column heading you wish to sort by.

It is possible to import customers from a data file, this is useful if you are moving from another accounting system and do not wish to enter all the supplier records manually into Sage Business Cloud Accounting. The process to do this is not described in this book, however if you wish to experiment with this you can create a data file using Microsoft Excel by downloading the template which you can access from the help page.

To access the supplier set up use   button and the customer set up page will open.

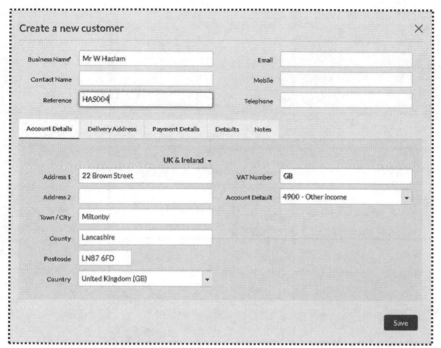

Enter the business name in the business name field, the account reference.

If the customer is VAT registered and you are aware of their VAT number this can be recorded here, as well as their bank account information. Feel free to complete these sections with some 'made up' information.

The Sales Ledger (Nominal) Account will default to Other Income Account 4900. This can be amended to the account you require but, for now, leave this unchanged.

Complete the contact information in the Addresses fields. Before you save the information you need to setup the Payment details. Click on 'Payment Details'.

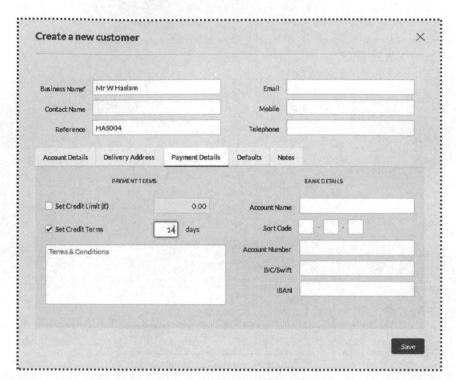

Place a tick in 'Set Credit Terms'. The default is 30 days. If the credit terms are not 30 days like above, you can amend accordingly. You may also in some situations have to add a credit limit which is just above.

Don't forget to SAVE!

 Activity

You have already entered one of TotalPhoto's customers (Mr W Haslam).

You should now enter the full details for each of the remaining five customers, and then save them to Sage Business Cloud Accounting.

Opening balance

As with the suppliers described in the previous chapter, you may need to enter an opening balance when setting up a new customer record. You can either do this now as part of a single set up or do them in one go for all the customers as was described for suppliers.

To set up an opening balance go to the summary screen, then from the getting started tab, select the 'Enter outstanding customer transaction option.

Set up customers

1. Create or import customers ❓
2. Enter money customers owe to you ❓
3. Review the Aged Debtors report

After selection you will be taken to the Customer Opening Balances page.

You will notice the 'Accounts Start Date' was set as 01/10/XX as the first day of the accounting period for the current year.

Using the [New Opening Balance] button – select New Opening Balance. Using the screen provided enter the opening balance for Mr W Haslam as shown below.

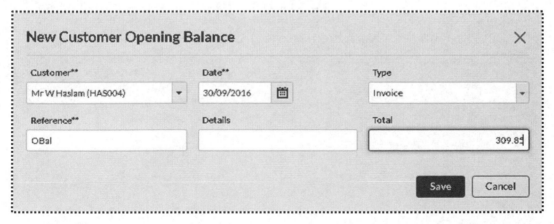

Use Invoice as the type, enter the 30th September 20XX, select Mr W Haslam. Opening Balances will always default to the last day of the previous financial year on Sage Business Cloud Accounting. This is acceptable and when producing reports later, you can widen the date range to include opening balances. Since we are not entering information for a particular invoice, the reference and details should be something to help you identify this as a transaction. Then save.

 Activity

You have already entered one of TotalPhoto's customers opening balances (Mr W Haslam).

You should now enter the opening balance for each of the remaining five customers and then save them to Sage Business Cloud Accounting.

When you have done this, the Customers Opening Balances page should look like this:

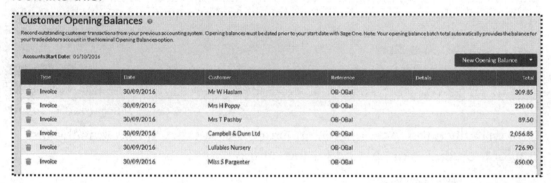

© Copyright Sage (UK) Limited 2018

3 Printing customer data reports

Customer data reports are available from the customer list page.

© Copyright Sage (UK) Limited 2018

From the 'Contacts' menu, select the Customers option, you will be taken to the customer list.

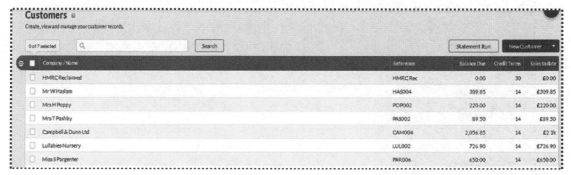

© Copyright Sage (UK) Limited 2018

You will notice from the image above there are some additional columns which are not displaying in your view. To add these columns using the

cog [image] and you will be able to select which columns are in view.

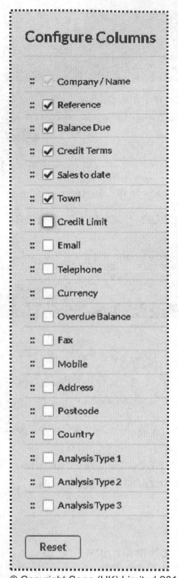

© Copyright Sage (UK) Limited 2018

De-select Email and Telephone and ensure the below are selected:

- Reference
- Balance Due
- Credit Terms
- Sales To Date
- Town

The column order can be changed, to re-order columns

click on the symbol ⠿ and drag the column to the required position.

To access the reports you will need to select the customers which are required to be included in the report. This is done by selecting them in the list using the tick boxes to the left of the customer name.

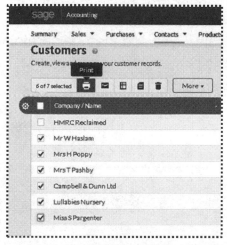

Having selected the customers you require, the customer reports can be accessed.

Using the toolbar:

Select the printer icon or pdf icon to send the customer list to a printable report format:

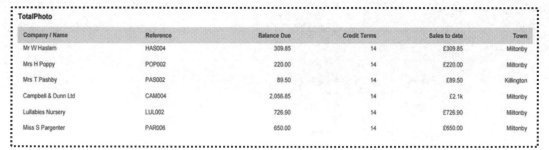

TotalPhoto					
Company / Name	Reference	Balance Due	Credit Terms	Sales to date	Town
Mr W Haslam	HAS004	309.85	14	£309.85	Miltonby
Mrs H Poppy	POP002	220.00	14	£220.00	Miltonby
Mrs T Pashby	PAS002	89.50	14	£89.50	Killington
Campbell & Dunn Ltd	CAM004	2,056.85	14	£2.1k	Miltonby
Lullabies Nursery	LUL002	726.90	14	£726.90	Miltonby
Miss S Pargenter	PAR006	650.00	14	£650.00	Miltonby

Using the More button [More ▾ / Activity Report / Address List / Statement Summary Report] select Address List, to view the list of selected customers with their address details. You will be asked which address types you require. You can select 'All' and then Generate.

To access the report, go to the black navigation bar reports icon to display available reports and click on the customer address list option.

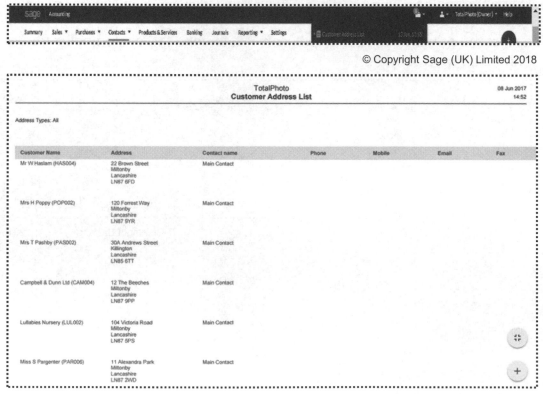

The nominal ledger

7

ASSESSMENT CRITERIA

Enter information relating to the organisation at the beginning of an accounting period (1.1)

Produce routine reports from the general ledger (5.2)

CONTENTS

1 Introduction

2 Set up and amend general ledger accounts

3 Enter the relevant opening balance information

4 Printing a trial balance

1 Introduction

The nominal ledger is probably the most important element of the Sage Business Cloud Accounting (or indeed any) accounting system. The key aspect to this is the list of nominal codes. This is simply a series of different accounts which are used each time a transaction is recorded.

Each of these accounts are given a unique four digit code number. To view the list of Nominal Codes go to the Chart of Accounts set up. Summary, then from the Getting started tab, Set up chart of accounts then 'Review the standard chart of accounts'.

© Copyright Sage (UK) Limited 2018

Set up chart of accounts

1. Review the standard chart of accounts ❷
2. Enter opening account balances ❷
3. Review the Trial Balance report ❷

© Copyright Sage (UK) Limited 2018

The four-digit code is important, as the list is broken down into groups:

0000–0999	Fixed Assets and Depreciation (e.g. Buildings, Equipment)
1000–1999	Current Assets (e.g. Stock, Debtors, Bank)
2000–2999	Current Liabilities (e.g. Loans, Creditors)
3000–3999	Equity, Capital and Reserves
4000–4999	Sales & Income
5000–5999	Direct Expenses (e.g. Purchases)
6000–6999	Overheads (e.g. Direct Labour)
7000–7999	Overheads (e.g. Phone, Rent, Postage, Wages)
8000–8999	General Expenses, Bad debts, Depreciation
9000–9999	Suspense and Mispostings

Sage Business Cloud Accounting uses these 'groupings' of codes to ensure that items appear in the correct part of the Income Statement or Statement of Financial Position. You may have heard of these financial statements referred to as a 'Profit and Loss Account' or 'Balance Sheet'. Don't worry you will not have to deal with these as part of your level 2 accounting qualification and will learn how to prepare these at the next level.

In Sage Business Cloud Accounting, you can easily amend the description of a nominal code, or indeed add a new one. However, you must always make sure that you keep the code in the correct 'grouping' for the type of account that it is.

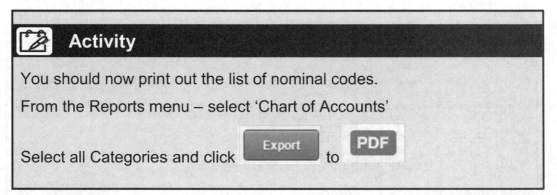

Activity

You should now print out the list of nominal codes.

From the Reports menu – select 'Chart of Accounts'

Select all Categories and click **Export** to **PDF**

Control accounts

There are some very special Nominal Codes called Control Accounts, which are essential to the running of the Sage Business Cloud Accounting software. **These cannot be deleted and are always present in the Chart of Accounts.**

Control accounts are used automatically by Sage Business Cloud Accounting. This means that you do not need to specify them individually when entering transactions – Sage Business Cloud Accounting will work out which control account is required and apply it automatically. Other Nominal Codes (from the list you printed out) will need to be entered.

Control Accounts include Trade Debtors Control and Trade Creditors Control, also referred to as SLCA and PLCA. These accounts will be used automatically when posting a sales or a purchase invoice for example, and will store the total amounts owing by customers and to suppliers.

The Bank Account is also a control account as are the accounts to which VAT is posted following sales and purchases. This enables accurate recording of VAT liability for completion of VAT returns.

2 Set up and amend general ledger accounts

The default Chart of Accounts contains the most common codes set up for a general business. However, you will almost certainly want to add to, or amend, these Nominal Codes to suit your business in particular.

For example, in your case study TotalPhoto you will want to be more specific when recording its sales and purchases. Before you do this, have a look at your listing of Nominal Codes. Find the 5000-5999 Range (remember, these are set aside for Purchases – category Direct Expenses).

From the reports menu, select Chart of Accounts List, select Category 'Direct Expenses' then search and the following list will appear:

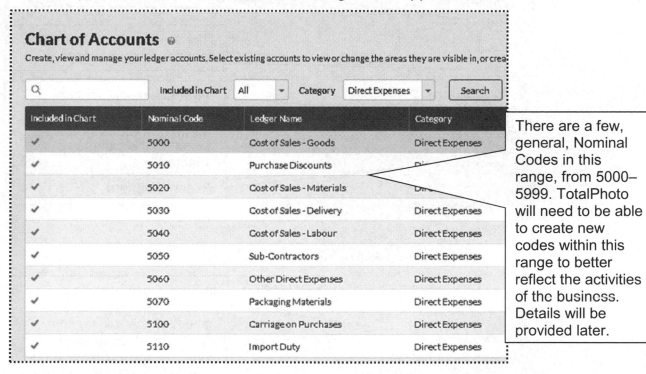

Chart of Accounts

Create, view and manage your ledger accounts. Select existing accounts to view or change the areas they are visible in, or crea

Included in Chart	Nominal Code	Ledger Name	Category
✓	5000	Cost of Sales - Goods	Direct Expenses
✓	5010	Purchase Discounts	Di
✓	5020	Cost of Sales - Materials	Di
✓	5030	Cost of Sales - Delivery	Direct Expenses
✓	5040	Cost of Sales - Labour	Direct Expenses
✓	5050	Sub-Contractors	Direct Expenses
✓	5060	Other Direct Expenses	Direct Expenses
✓	5070	Packaging Materials	Direct Expenses
✓	5100	Carriage on Purchases	Direct Expenses
✓	5110	Import Duty	Direct Expenses

There are a few, general, Nominal Codes in this range, from 5000–5999. TotalPhoto will need to be able to create new codes within this range to better reflect the activities of the business. Details will be provided later.

To create a new nominal code or amend an existing code, go to settings in the main screen, select Chart of Accounts then click **New Ledger Account** and the following set up screen will appear:

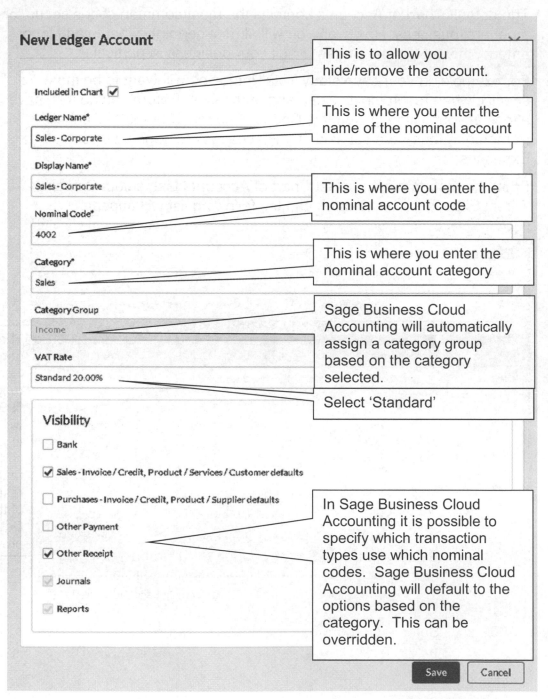

New Ledger Account

This is to allow you hide/remove the account.

Included in Chart ✓

This is where you enter the name of the nominal account

Ledger Name*
Sales - Corporate

Display Name*
Sales - Corporate

Nominal Code*
4002

This is where you enter the nominal account code

Category*
Sales

This is where you enter the nominal account category

Category Group
Income

Sage Business Cloud Accounting will automatically assign a category group based on the category selected.

VAT Rate
Standard 20.00%

Select 'Standard'

Visibility

☐ Bank

✓ Sales - Invoice / Credit, Product / Services / Customer defaults

☐ Purchases - Invoice / Credit, Product / Supplier defaults

☐ Other Payment

✓ Other Receipt

✓ Journals

✓ Reports

In Sage Business Cloud Accounting it is possible to specify which transaction types use which nominal codes. Sage Business Cloud Accounting will default to the options based on the category. This can be overridden.

Save   Cancel

To amend an existing nominal account from the Chart of Accounts set up screen, select the account with a mouse click, the edit screen will appear. Make edits as required.

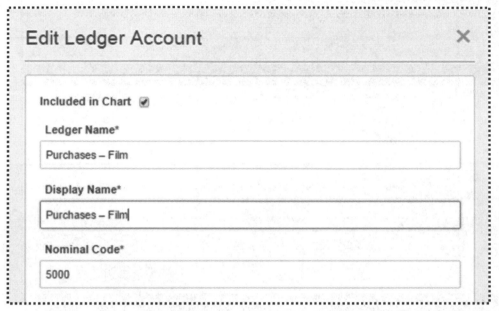

 Activity

To practice amending and creating Nominal Codes (N/Cs), enter each of the following N/Cs and names. Do them one by one and then save each one, the VAT rate should be standard 20%. These are all relevant to our case study firm and– TotalPhoto.

SALES		PURCHASES (Direct Expenses)	
Nominal Code	Name	Nominal Code	Name
4000	Sales – Individuals & Family	5000	Purchases – Film
4001	Sales – Weddings	5001	Purchases – Paper
4002	Sales – Corporate	5002	Purchases – Cartridges & Toner
4003	Sales – Nurseries & Schools	5003	Purchases – Stationery
4004	Other sales	5004	Purchases – Other Consumables

When you have finished; re-run the Chart of Accounts report to check that all your additions and amendments have been made correctly.

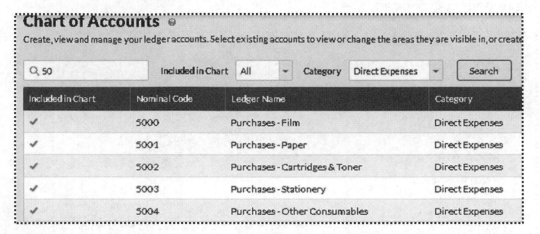

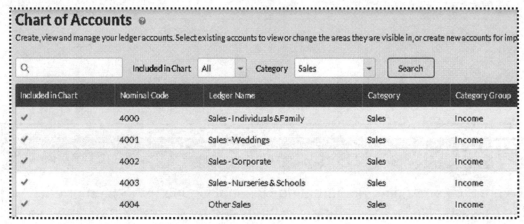

The next step is to post opening balances to each relevant nominal code within Sage Business Cloud Accounting for your business.

KAPLAN PUBLISHING

Activity

You now need to enter the opening balances for each of the accounts relating to TotalPhoto. These will be the balance on each account at the end of the previous accounting period, so on 30th September 20XX. The list of opening balances is shown on the next page and **detailed guidance on how to enter these balances and follow this activity.**

Important

1   You will need to create new Nominal Codes for two items: Photographic Equipment (std rate VAT 20%) and Photographic Equipment Depreciation (NO VAT and use Fixed Assets for the category when setting up the new codes). You may also choose to re-name the nominal account Capital Introduced (no 3200) to Capital – These need entering/updating **before** going to the opening balances screen.

2   You do not need to enter opening balances for two items, the Trade Debtors Control Account and the Trade Creditors Control Account. This is because these represent the total amount owed to us (debtors/receivables) and the total amount we owe (creditors/payables), made up of all of the individual balances you entered earlier. These control account balances are therefore calculated automatically by Sage Business Cloud Accounting and **you do not enter them.**

3   The cash and bank balances will be entered first. Cash can be changed to Cash in Hand (no 1210). Current can be changed to Bank (no 1200).

4   Be very careful to enter each balance correctly as either a **debit** or a **credit** balance. Take your time to complete this activity as it will help prevent you making errors at this stage.

5   Remember you can edit any of the account names and create any relevant nominal codes. It is recommended that you run through the nominal codes and names before you enter the opening balances to ensure that the details are as you want them to be.

TotalPhoto

Opening balances

	Nominal code	Debit	Credit
Motor vehicles (at cost)	0050	21800.00	
Motor Vehicles Depreciation	0051		5450.00
Office Equipment	0030	4849.00	
Office Equipment Depreciation	0031		921.00
Photographic Equipment	0032	22718.00	
Photographic Equip Depreciation	0033		4316.00
Stock (as at 1st October 20XX)	1000	7403.00	
Cash in Hand	*1210*	**250.00**	
Bank	*1200*	**10293.00**	
Trade Creditors Control Account	2100		19192.41
Capital	3200		20000.00
Purchases – Film	5000	205.63	
Purchases – Paper	5001	1034.35	
Purchases – Cartridges & Toner	5002	1225.87	
Purchases – Stationery	5003	409.35	
Purchases – Other Consumables	5004	823.52	
Sales – Individuals & Families	4000		5401.21
Sales – Weddings	4001		3984.50
Sales – Corporate	4002		1932.09
Sales – Nurseries & Schools	4003		11304.20
Other Sales	4004		1590.30
Rent & Rates	7100	4280.00	
Office Costs	7520	603.43	
Motor expenses	7340	1035.64	
Travel & Entertainment	7400	229.39	
Trade Debtors Control Account	1100	4053.10	
Profit & Loss	3100		5498.28
VAT	2202		1623.29
		81213.28	**81213.28**

Note: this is the total of the suppliers' balances that you entered earlier. This has already been entered and so will not need to be entered again

Similarly this is the total of the individual customers' accounts that you entered earlier. Again, this will not need to be entered again

3 Enter the relevant opening balance information

Entering opening balances in Sage Business Cloud Accounting is very straightforward. If you enter an opening balance incorrectly, you can easily change the entry in the screen below.

From the 'Summary page' (Home page), 'Set up Chart of accounts' select

> ② **Enter opening account balances** ❷

And the following screen will appear. The date must be left as 30/09/20XX as Sage Business Cloud Accounting defaults to the last day of the previous financial year for any opening balances. You will notice the opening balances on the Trade debtors and Trade creditors control account will already be entered. This has come from the opening balances entered earlier for suppliers and customers.

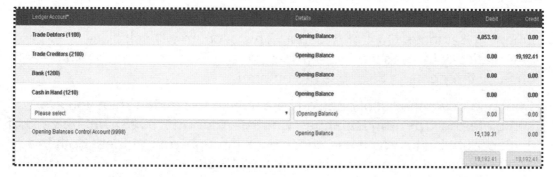

Bank and Cash in Hand opening balances

We will enter the Bank and Cash in Hand balances first. Click on the Line for the Bank account code 1200, enter the relevant details then repeat for code 1210, click save.

We can now go back to enter all other opening balances from the list. Go to:

© Copyright Sage (UK) Limited 2018

© Copyright Sage (UK) Limited 2018

Enter the balances date and from the next available line select nominal Motor Vehicles – Cost (0050) and enter a debit value of £21,800.

You will notice a balancing figure will be displayed automatically in the Opening Balances Control Account. This account will calculate automatically to keep the system 'in-balance'. This account should be zero once all the opening balances are entered.

Continue down the list of opening balances to the end. When you are complete **the Opening Balances Control Account (9998) will be zero**. If this account isn't zero please check back through your entries. Both the debit and credit column should equal 81,213.28.

© Copyright Sage (UK) Limited 2018

Once you have entered all of the nominal account opening balances, including cash and bank balances, together with the supplier and customer balances, the opening balances process is complete. You can click Save.

4 Printing a trial balance

You should now have entered all the opening balances for TotalPhoto. You are now ready to begin entering transactions on a day to day basis. Before you do this, you should print off a Trial Balance.

 Activity

Print off a trial balance for TotalPhoto as at 30 September 20XX. Guidance on how to do this follows.

From the Reporting Menu – select 'Trial Balance'

Select balances from 30th September 20XX to 30th September 20XX and don't forget to click 'Calculate'.

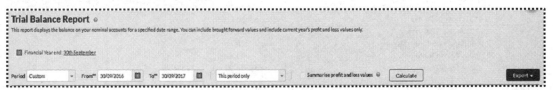

View on screen, export to pdf or Excel as shown below:

From	30/03/2016	To	30/03/2017
Nominal Code	Name	Selected Period	
		Debit	Credit
30	Office equipment - Cost	4,849.00	
31	Office equipment - Accumulated Depreciation		321
32	Photographic Equipment	22,718.00	
33	Photographic Equip Depreciation		4,316.00
50	Motor Vehicles - Cost	21,800.00	
51	Motor Vehicles - Accumulated Depreciation		5,450.00
1000	Stock	7,403.00	
1100	Trade Debtors	4,053.10	
1200	Bank	10,293.00	
1210	Cash in Hand	250	
2100	Trade Creditors		19,192.41
2202	VAT Liability		1,623.23
3100	Profit and Loss Account		5,438.28
3200	Capital introduced		20,000.00
4000	Sales - Individuals &Family		5,401.21
4001	Sales - Weddings		3,384.50
4002	Sales - Corporate		1,332.03
4003	Sales - Nurseries & Schools		11,304.20
4004	Other Sales		1,530.30
5000	Purchases - Film	205.63	
5001	Purchases - Paper	1,034.35	
5002	Purchases - Cartridges & Toner	1,225.87	
5003	Purchases - Stationery	409.35	
5004	Purchases - Other Consumables	823.52	
7100	Rent & Rates	4,280.00	
7340	Motor Expenses	1,035.64	
7400	Travel & Entertainment	223.33	
7520	Office Costs	603.43	
	TOTAL	£81,213.28	£81,213.28

How to amend an incorrect opening balance

If any of the balances are different to the ones on your printed version, you are able to amend as follows:

Firstly tick off your trial balance to determine which opening balances have been entered incorrectly and make a note of them.

If you find any errors – return to the opening balances screen and edit accordingly.

Entering transactions

<table>
<tr><td>

ASSESSMENT CRITERIA

Process sales invoices and credit notes (2.1)

Allocate receipts from customers (2.2)

Process purchase invoices and credit notes (2.3)

Allocate payments to suppliers (2.4)

Process receipts and payments for non-credit transactions (3.1)

Process petty cash receipts and payments (3.3)

Produce routine reports for customers and suppliers (5.1)

Produce routine reports from the general ledger (5.2)

</td><td>

CONTENTS

1 Introduction

2 Credit sales – entering customer invoices

3 Customer credit notes

4 Producing customer statements

5 Credit purchases – entering supplier invoices

6 Supplier credit notes

7 Bank transactions

8 Making payments by BACS and cheque

9 Remittance advices

10 Recording receipts

11 Receipts from customers

12 Checking bank activity

13 Transfers

14 Petty cash

</td></tr>
</table>

1 Introduction

Any business will carry out a wide range of transactions every day of the week. However, the majority of these will fall into one of the following categories:

Credit transactions

- Purchases of inventory/stock on credit.
- Sales of goods or services on credit.

Cash transactions

- Purchases made by cash/cheque/card.
- Sales made for cash/cheque/card.
- Payments made to suppliers (for goods/services bought on credit).
- Receipts from customers (for goods/services sold on credit).
- Payments made to meet other expenses.
- Payment of salaries and wages to staff.
- Petty cash transactions.
- Transactions directly through the bank account (e.g. bank charges, interest, direct debits, standing orders).

Each of these transactions will have an effect on two accounts within the Sage Business Cloud Accounting system – this is the underlying principle of double-entry bookkeeping. However, Sage Business Cloud Accounting simplifies this by carrying out much of the double entry automatically.

Consider first the first transactions listed above – purchases and sales made on credit. This means that a legally binding contract is established between the two parties, and (usually) the goods or services are supplied but payment is not made until some later date. The key document in this process is the **invoice** – as this is the document which demands payment and lays down the agreed terms of the transaction.

Hence, entering a credit transaction (whether a purchase or a sale) is a two stage process in Sage Business Cloud Accounting.

(1) Enter the details of the invoice against the relevant supplier or customer. This will establish the presence and value of the legally binding debt.

(2) At a later date, enter the details of the payment of the debt, either the payment sent to the supplier or the receipt received from the customer.

Note that this approach is applicable for both credit sales and credit purchases – you just have to be sure to enter the details in the correct part of Sage Business Cloud Accounting.

Now consider the second set of transactions listed at the start of this Chapter – each of these has a direct impact on the bank accounts within Sage Business Cloud Accounting.

2 Credit sales – entering customer invoices

Our case study company TotalPhoto have had a number of credit customers. Each of these have been issued with an invoice, and these invoices now need to be entered into Sage Business Cloud Accounting.

The easiest way to do this is to **batch** invoices together so that they can be input at the same time.

To enter a batch of customer (sales) invoices go to the Sales tab and select 'Quick Entries'

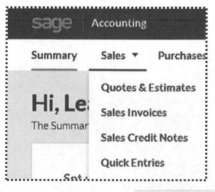

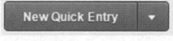

The transaction type – select INV for invoices

The Nominal Code to define what was sold. Remember, this will be a four digit number beginning with 4 that was either created by Sage Business Cloud Accounting or set up by yourself

Net value of invoice

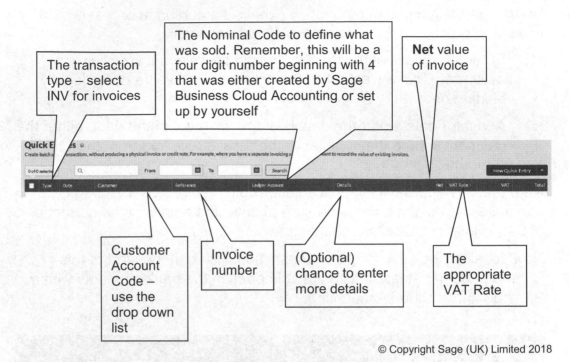

Customer Account Code – use the drop down list

Invoice number

(Optional) chance to enter more details

The appropriate VAT Rate

© Copyright Sage (UK) Limited 2018

Once you have entered all invoices in the batch you should then review

them to ensure you have entered them correctly, and then **Save** them. This will post the invoices to Sage Business Cloud Accounting and update the system accordingly.

If you wish to produce an Invoice document directly from Sage Business Cloud Accounting, and make the required posting simultaneously – take a look at the Sales Invoice creation option. Look at the in-built help screens if you need further guidance.

Activity

Enter the following six invoices for TotalPhoto using the Quick-entry screen. Note that you will also have to create new customer accounts in some cases. **It is advisable to do this before you start entering details of the invoices.**

Date	Invoice No	A/c No	Customer	Nominal Code	Net Amount
01/10/20XX	1	POP002	Poppy	4000	£105.00
01/10/20XX	2	HAS004	Haslam	4000	£24.50
01/10/20XX	3	PAR006	Pargenter	4000	£12.00
01/10/20XX	4	SMI009	Smith *(see below)*	4001	£600.00
01/10/20XX	5	LUL002	Lullabies Nursery	4003	£100.00
01/10/20XX	6	CAM004	Campbell & Dunn	4002	£45.00
01/10/20XX	7	HAS004	Haslam	4000	£12.00

All amounts in the table are **exclusive** of VAT at 20%

New Customer Details

Mr A Smith
12 Main Street
Miltonby
Lancashire
LN87 4DF

A/c Ref SMI009

Credit terms: Payment in 14 days

Credit Limit: £1000.00

Enter the details in the batch customer invoices screen as shown below. You can choose suitable wording for the 'details' field.

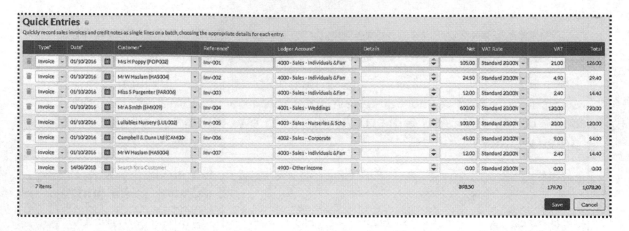

Quick Entries

Quickly record sales invoices and credit notes as single lines on a batch, choosing the appropriate details for each entry.

Type*	Date*	Customer*	Reference*	Ledger Account*	Details	Net	VAT Rate	VAT	Total
Invoice	01/10/2016	Mrs H Poppy (POP002)	Inv-001	4000 - Sales - Individuals & Fam		105.00	Standard 20.00%	21.00	126.00
Invoice	01/10/2016	Mr W Haslam (HAS004)	Inv-002	4000 - Sales - Individuals & Fam		24.50	Standard 20.00%	4.90	29.40
Invoice	01/10/2016	Miss S Pargenter (PAR006)	Inv-003	4000 - Sales - Individuals & Fam		12.00	Standard 20.00%	2.40	14.40
Invoice	01/10/2016	Mr A Smith (SMI009)	Inv-004	4001 - Sales - Weddings		600.00	Standard 20.00%	120.00	720.00
Invoice	01/10/2016	Lullabies Nursery (LUL002)	Inv-005	4003 - Sales - Nurseries & Scho		100.00	Standard 20.00%	20.00	120.00
Invoice	01/10/2016	Campbell & Ouns Ltd (CAM00	Inv-006	4002 - Sales - Corporate		45.00	Standard 20.00%	9.00	54.00
Invoice	01/10/2016	Mr W Haslam (HAS004)	Inv-007	4000 - Sales - Individuals & Fam		12.00	Standard 20.00%	2.40	14.40
Invoice	14/06/2018	Search for a Customer		4900 - Other Income		0.00	Standard 20.00%	0.00	0.00

7 items   898.50   179.70   1,078.20

Save   Cancel

When you have entered all seven invoices, your screen should look like this. Check for accuracy, and when you are happy press the

 button.

You will need to set up new customers ahead of entering the invoice for new customers when using this method of entry. This can be done at any time and added to the quick-entry batch.

 **Activity**

Print out another trial balance for 30th September 20XX to 1st October 20XX . Compare this with the one you prepared earlier and identify the changes that have occurred.

Here is a copy of how the Trial Balance should look now. Put the two reports side-by-side and note down the change on each nominal account.

From: 30/09/2016
To: 01/10/2016

TotalPhoto
Trial Balance Report

19 Jun 2018
21:18

This period only

Nominal Code	Name	Debit	Credit
0030	Office equipment - Cost	4,849.00	
0031	Office equipment - Accumulated Depreciation		921.00
0032	Photographic Equipment	22,718.00	
0033	Photographic Equip Depreciation		4,316.00
0050	Motor Vehicles - Cost	21,800.00	
0051	Motor Vehicles - Accumulated Depreciation		5,450.00
1000	Stock	7,403.00	
1100	Trade Debtors	5,131.30	
1200	Bank	10,293.00	
1210	Cash in Hand	250.00	
2100	Trade Creditors		19,192.41
2200	VAT on Sales		179.70
2202	VAT Liability		1,623.29
3100	Profit and Loss Account		5,498.28
3200	Capital introduced		20,000.00
4000	Sales - Individuals &Family		5,554.71
4001	Sales - Weddings		4,584.50
4002	Sales - Corporate		1,977.09
4003	Sales - Nurseries & Schools		11,404.20
4004	Other Sales		1,590.30
5000	Purchases - Film	205.63	
5001	Purchases - Paper	1,034.35	
5002	Purchases - Cartridges & Toner	1,225.87	
5003	Purchases - Stationery	409.35	
5004	Purchases - Other Consumables	823.52	
7100	Rent & Rates	4,280.00	
7340	Motor Expenses	1,035.64	
7400	Travel & Entertainment	229.39	
7520	Office Costs	603.43	
	TOTAL	£82,291.48	£82,291.48

Notice which figures have changed

(1) N/C 1100 (Debtors control account) has increased from £4053.10 to £5131.30. This reflects the fact that TotalPhoto is now owed an additional £1078.20 by its debtors/receivables.

(2) N/Cs 4000, 4001, 4002 and 4003 have increased, representing the new sales that the company made on 30th September. Note that the increase in these figures (£898.50) is the **net** increase in sales.

(3) There is a new Nominal Code (2200) called 'VAT on Sales'. This account automatically records output VAT (on sales) and is used to calculate and produce the company's VAT Return. The amount on this code is currently £179.70 (a **credit** balance) – the VAT charged on all the sales invoices you have entered.

If you would like to see the 'movement' in more detail, i.e. viewing how the balances have changed from the opening balances position until now – try running the Nominal Activity Report for the same period of time – for the selected accounts. Here is the activity for the sales accounts:

© Copyright Sage (UK) Limited 2018

4003 - Sales - Nurseries & Schools

Tix	Date	Inv No	Name	Type	Reference	Description	Debit	Credit	Running Total
						Opening Balance:		0.00	
15	30/09/2016			Journal Opening Balance	Opening Balances	(Opening Balance)		11,304.20	11,304.20 Cr
20	01/10/2016		Lullabies Nursery (LUL002)	Sales QE Invoice	Inv-005			100.00	11,404.20 Cr
						Totals:	0.00	11,404.20	
						Closing Balance:		11,404.20	
						Period Variance:		11,404.20	

4004 - Other Sales

Tix	Date	Inv No	Name	Type	Reference	Description	Debit	Credit	Running Total
						Opening Balance:		0.00	
15	30/09/2016			Journal Opening Balance	Opening Balances	(Opening Balance)		1,590.30	1,590.30 Cr
						Totals:	0.00	1,590.30	
						Closing Balance:		1,590.30	
						Period Variance:		1,590.30	

3 Customer credit notes

A credit note is essentially a 'negative invoice' and is produced and sent to customers when a refund is needed. The most likely time this will happen is when goods that the organisation has sold to a customer have been returned as faulty. However, they can also be used to correct errors.

Producing a credit note in Sage Business Cloud Accounting is straightforward and can be done in three ways depending on the method the original invoice was originally created.

(1) If Invoices are created within Sage Business Cloud Accounting using the 'Sales Invoice' function, whereby an invoice document is generated and sent directly from the system, a Credit Note can be made from the Invoice in question and then modified to reflect the amount of credit agreed. This could be 100% of the Invoice value or just a proportion, depending on the circumstances. By creating a Credit Note this way, the Credit Note and the Invoice to which it relates will be linked or allocated together, making the customer statements easier to understand.

(2) Credit Notes can also be created in a similar way to Invoices using the 'Sales Credit Notes' function and can either be allocated to an invoice as a later operation or just left on the account as independent transactions, forming part of the outstanding balance, or refund due.

(3) In this text we will describe Credit Note transactions, assuming the document itself has been created outside of Sage Business Cloud Accounting, in the same way we posted customer invoices earlier – using the 'Sales Quick Entry' screen.

Activity

Let us suppose that the sale of a 6" × 4" colour print made by TotalPhoto to Miss Pargenter for £12.00 (plus VAT) (Invoice No 3) is returned as faulty. It is necessary to issue a credit note so that this debt is effectively 'removed' from Miss Pargenter's account. Enter the credit note on Sage Business Cloud Accounting. Guidance on how to enter it follows. Date the Credit 8th October 20XX.

How to process a customer credit note

To enter a customer (sales) credit go to the Sales tab and select 'Quick Entries'

© Copyright Sage (UK) Limited 2018

The transaction type – select Cr note for credits

The Nominal Code to define what was sold. Remember, this will be a four digit number beginning with 4 that was either created by Sage Business Cloud Accounting or set up by yourself

Net Amount of Credit

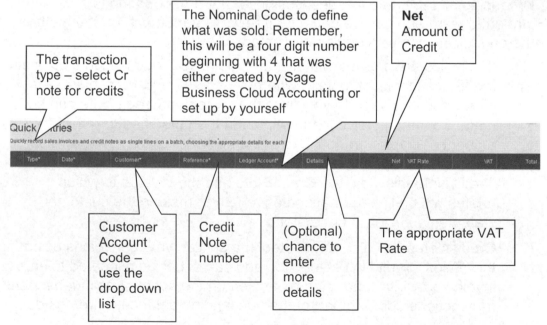

Customer Account Code – use the drop down list

Credit Note number

(Optional) chance to enter more details

The appropriate VAT Rate

© Copyright Sage (UK) Limited 2018

Once you have entered the credit, you should . This will post the credit to Sage Business Cloud Accounting and update the system accordingly.

Viewing a Customer's Account

From the Customer List, locate 'Miss S Pargenter' either by using the search or filter features or simply visually scanning down the list and click on the line.

This will take you to the record of 'Miss S Pargenter'.

We want to view the activity to this account so once in the record, scroll down to the bottom to find this section:

Enter 30/9/20XX in the 'From' field and 30/9/20XX in the 'To' field. You will be able to view all the activity that has taken place on this account between those two points in time. Additional filters around transaction types and status can also be used to refine the view and if required print or email the view displayed. This can be accessed by clicking 'Type' or the 'Status' field.

You will be able to see the opening balance and the invoices and credits already posted. Other transactions that could appear here include, payments received and refunds made – which will be covered later in this text.

All transactions on a customer account will have their original values plus a balance i.e. the amount of the transaction that has not been paid or refunded.

To allocate the invoice [INV-003] to the credit note [CRN-002] follow the steps described below:

From the customer record scroll back to the top and using the

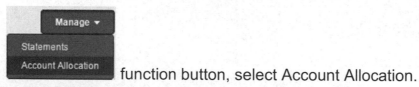 function button, select Account Allocation.

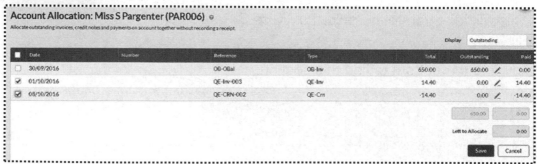

Using the selector tick boxes, select both the credit note and the invoice and save.

The customer activity should now look like this:

Date	Number	Reference	Type	Total	Discount	Outstanding
30/09/2016	OBal		Customer OB Invoice	650.00		650.00
01/10/2016	INV-003		Sales QE Invoice	14.40		0.00
08/10/2016			Customer Allocation	0.00		0.00
08/10/2016	CRN-002		Sales QE Credit	-14.40		0.00

The account balance has not changed overall, but the individual balances of the transactions have – in this case INV-003 and CRN-002 have a fully allocated balance of zero. Please note the date column can be clicked to show the transactions in date order.

4 Producing customer statements

Having produced and sent invoices to customers, most businesses will also need to send periodic (usually monthly) statements to their customers which will list all new transactions – such as their new purchases, payments sent, credit notes issued to them etc.

Sage Business Cloud Accounting allows the easy creation and production of customer statements.

The format of the customer statement that will be produced is based on the invoice template design style found in the settings area. The default template can be used and you do not need to change it.

From the customer list select the customer that you wish to either send a statement to or to set up periodic auto-mated email schedule for. Normally this process would be done when the customer account is initially set up.

Click on Miss S Pargenter

From the customer record screen, using the function button, select Statements.

In the statements screen you will be able to see the balance owed – £650.

If you set the date to 8th October 20XX then hit the calculate button, you will see the invoice outstanding in the activity list as shown. You can see how easy it is to select the relevant statement date.

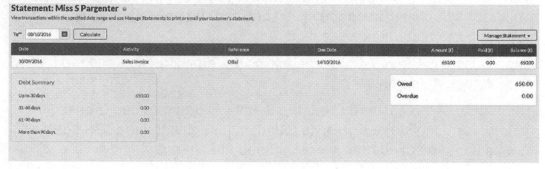

Using the Manage Statement function button you will be able to:

Send to pdf or csv for printing

Email a statement directly to the customer. The email address will autofill if it has been added to the contact record

Set up the email and postal addresses and create a recurring automated statement schedule

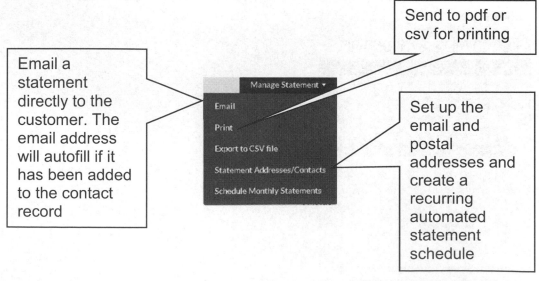

Activity

Create and print a customer statement for Miss Pargenter (Ref PAR006)
It should look like this:

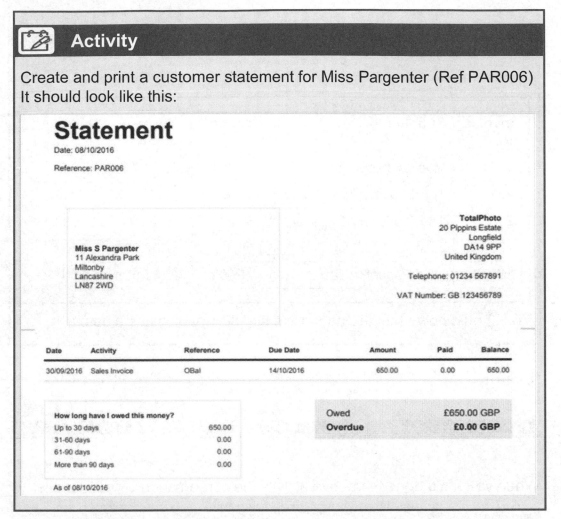

Statement

Date: 08/10/2016

Reference: PAR006

Miss S Pargenter
11 Alexandra Park
Miltonby
Lancashire
LN87 2WD

TotalPhoto
20 Pippins Estate
Longfield
DA14 9PP
United Kingdom

Telephone: 01234 567891

VAT Number: GB 123456789

Date	Activity	Reference	Due Date	Amount	Paid	Balance
30/09/2016	Sales Invoice	OBal	14/10/2016	650.00	0.00	650.00

How long have I owed this money?	
Up to 30 days	650.00
31-60 days	0.00
61-90 days	0.00
More than 90 days	0.00

Owed	£650.00 GBP
Overdue	**£0.00 GBP**

As of 08/10/2016

5 Credit purchases – entering supplier invoices

When an organisation purchases goods or services on credit, it will receive an invoice from the supplier. These must be recorded immediately in Sage Business Cloud Accounting, even though they may not be paid for some time. This is when the business has purchased on credit, i.e. to pay later.

The most common way to process supplier invoices is to **batch** them (in much the same way as you did with the invoices to customers). This way, a number of invoices can be processed at the same time.

The process for entering batches of supplier statements is very similar to that for entering batches of customer invoices – except it is accessed via the Purchases tab.

Activity

TotalPhoto received the following five invoices on 1st October 20XX.

Invoice Ref	Supplier	Account	Net amount	Nominal Code
1341	Mackay Films	MF001	£208.76	5000
209	The Stationery Cupboard	SC003	£14.65	5003
216	The Stationery Cupboard	SC003	£78.92	5003
2203	Octopus Inks Ltd	OI001	£309.28	5002
10092	Mills Paper Products	MP002	£162.52	5001

You should now enter the above five supplier invoices as a batch.

When you have done the above activity the screen should look like this:

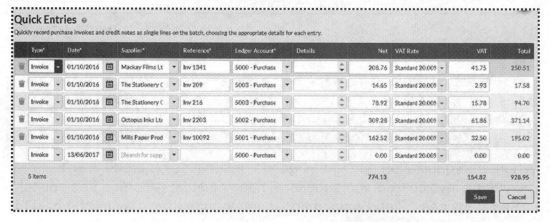

You should verify the entries and then press the [Save] button to post your entries to Sage Business Cloud Accounting.

You will be returned to the Quick Entry screen upon saving. If you wish to review the batch – refine the dates to include 1st October 20XX.

6 Supplier credit notes

These are processed in exactly the same way as you processed credit notes issued to customers.

Access the entry screen from the Purchases tab.

 Activity

TotalPhoto receives one credit note. It is from Arthur's Photographic Equipment Ltd (Ref AP004) and is a credit for £2,109.99 (NO VAT – we will ignore VAT for this activity). The credit is for a camera that was returned as faulty. The credit note reference is 134C and the date is 8th October 20XX . The Nominal Code for this is 0032 (Fixed Asset – Photographic Equipment). Process the credit note using a suitable narrative for the details section (a suggestion has been shown).

Before you carry out this activity, you need to ensure that the nominal account 0032 is **visible in the Purchases area** of Sage Business Cloud Accounting. Using the Chart of Accounts set up as described earlier in this text, edit ledger account 0032 as shown below:

Your entry screen for the above activity should look like this:

Don't forget to **Save** .

7   Bank transactions

Sage Business Cloud Accounting allows you to run a number of 'bank accounts'. These need not necessarily all be held at a bank – they could also include cash in hand, petty cash etc.

The principles for making payments in or out of any of these accounts are the same.

From the Banking tab, you can see that Sage Business Cloud Accounting has already set up two different bank accounts, each with its own Nominal Code. You can of course amend these or add to them if you wish.

The most commonly used bank account is probably Nominal Code 1200 (Bank Current Account). This is the one that you will use in this case study for payments in and out of TotalPhoto's main current account. You can see that it has a balance at the moment of £10,293.00. You may recall that this relates to the opening balance that you entered earlier. **None of the entries that you have made since then have affected the bank balance**.

8   Making payments by BACS and cheque

A business will need to make regular payments, either by cash, cheque or by BACS payment. The most common transaction will be when a business pays its suppliers when they have previously bought on credit (promised to pay later). However, they may simply need to pay for day to day expenses. We can now look at the process of entering these types of payments in Sage Business Cloud Accounting.

9   Remittance advices

It is common for businesses to produce a remittance advice when raising payments to suppliers. This document would notify the supplier of any invoices that are being paid and also any credit notes that have been taken into account when making the payment. It is a simple exercise to raise a remittance advice and guidance follows.

 Activity

TotalPhoto has three payments to make on 1st October 20XX. These are:

- a cheque for £107.65 (plus VAT at 20.0%) to Arrow Telecoms to pay the telephone bill

- a cheque for £55.00 to Miltonby Cricket Association for advertising in their League Handbook (no VAT on this transaction – Exempt)

- a cheque for £45.00 to Miltonby Borough Council for a parking permit (no VAT – Zero Rated).

Enter the above transactions on to Sage Business Cloud Accounting. We will look at how to produce a remittance in the next activity.

Click the New Entry

then– Purchase/Payment within the 'Bank' screen.

Using the 'Other Payment' tab area, enter the payment details one at a time for each payment. These payments are not related to a pre-existing Supplier invoice in the system and therefore the Supplier details are optional. 'Arrow Telecoms' has been typed in to the Supplier field. Select the 'method' of payment and be careful to make sure you select the appropriate Nominal Code for the expense item, and also the correct VAT rate.

The total amount should be entered first INCLUSIVE of VAT and then analysed. The VAT will calculate automatically based on the VAT Rate selected.

[The payment amount to Arrow Telecoms is £107.65 + 20% = £129.18]

Where a payment is for more than one category of items, it is possible to analyse the payment across multiple nominal codes. In this case it's for just one – Office Costs. If there are multiple lines – Sage Business Cloud Accounting will display the amount 'left to record' which must be zero before you are able to save. An example might be the purchase of fuel and food from the same supplier in one transaction. You would need to enter the fuel to one nominal code and the food to another.

Save each transaction separately. To add a new transaction having entered one – take advantage of the 'Add Another' function. We are unable to produce a remittance for 'other payments'.

You could also include extra optional details such as the cheque number or BACS in the '**Ref**' box.

Now check the balance on Nominal Code 1200 (the bank current account).

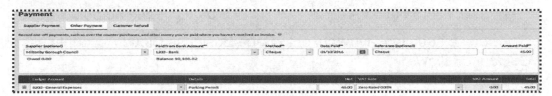

See how the bank balance has now gone down to **£10,063.82** – reflecting the fact that payments of £229.18 (£207.65 plus £21.53 VAT) have been taken from it.

Paying suppliers

We can now look at the other common area for payments which is paying suppliers when the business has previously bought goods on credit. This is especially common for buying inventory/stock.

 Activity

TotalPhoto also decides to pay two outstanding creditors on 1st October 20XX, as follows:

The Stationery Cupboard (SC003)
Amount: £375 inc VAT   *Paid by cheque number 00245*

K2 Films Ltd (KF001)
Amount £1726.55 (inc VAT).   *Paid by cheque number 00246*

Enter these supplier payments onto Sage Business Cloud Accounting. Guidance follows.

Click the [image] New Entry – Purchase/Payment within the 'Bank' screen.

Using the 'Supplier Payment' tab area, enter the payment details one at a time for each payment. These payments will be related to a pre-existing supplier invoice in the system and therefore the Supplier details are mandatory.

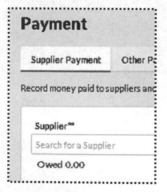

© Copyright Sage (UK) Limited 2018

✓   Type 'The Stationery Cupboard' into the Supplier field

✓   Select Bank Account: Current (code 1200)

✓   Enter Payment Date: 1st October 20XX

✓   Enter the Cheque number into the reference field

The account balance (£487.28) and related outstanding invoices will appear automatically at the bottom of the screen in the activity list.

✓   Enter the amount in the 'Amount Paid' field

✓   From the activity list, select the invoices you are wishing to pay

✓   Check the total amount is the amount you are wishing to pay

✓   Check 'Left to allocate' is zero

NB It is also possible in Sage Business Cloud Accounting to make 'payments on account' and make 'part payments' of invoices.

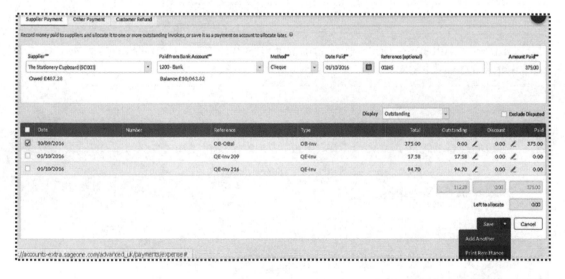

Once the payment details are entered you can either 'Save and Add Another' or 'Save and Print a Remittance'. Here is what the remittance should look like:

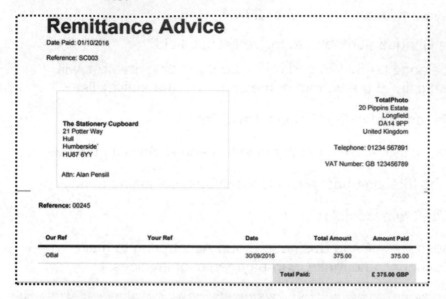

© Copyright Sage (UK) Limited 2018

NB: if the remittance does not appear, it is likely your browser is blocking a pop-up. To unblock:

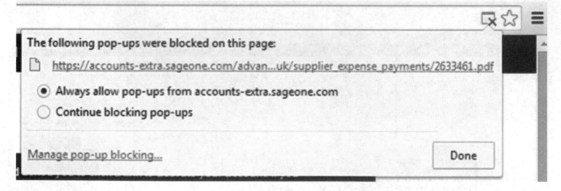

© Copyright Sage (UK) Limited 2018

Now enter the next payment to K2 Films Ltd, in the same way

© Copyright Sage (UK) Limited 2018

KAPLAN PUBLISHING

10 Recording receipts

The most likely sources of receipts for most businesses are:

- cash sales

- receipts from Trade Debtors/Receivables which are customers who have previously bought goods on credit.

We will look at these in turn.

Cash sales

These are transactions that relate to sales made for cash rather than on credit. The funds are received immediately by the business in the form of cash, cheque or card.

 Activity

TotalPhoto also sells items to two customers who pay cash on 1st October. The first of these is a 6" × 4" Colour Print for £12.00 plus VAT (use nominal code 4000); the second is for School Photos (Set 2) for £28.00 plus VAT of 20% (nominal code 4003).

Enter these cash sales into the bank current account on Sage Business Cloud Accounting. Detailed guidance follows.

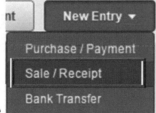

Click the New Entry – Sale within the 'Bank Screen'

Using the Other Receipt tab area, enter the receipt details one at a time for each receipt. These receipts are not related to a pre-existing Customer invoice in the system and therefore the Customer details are optional. Be careful to make sure you select the appropriate Nominal Code for the expense item, and also the correct VAT rate.

The total amount should be entered first INCLUSIVE of VAT and then analysed. The VAT will calculate automatically based on the VAT Rate selected. We can enter the TOTAL amount of both receipts £48. In the 'Amount Received' field.

Then enter each line:

[The receipt amount from Customer 1 is £12.00 + 20% = £14.40]

[The receipt amount from Customer 2 is £28.00 + 20% = £33.60]

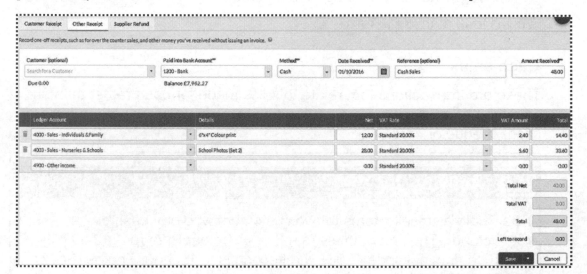

Click the **SAVE** button to post your entries to Sage Business Cloud Accounting.

 **Receipts from customers**

Businesses will regularly receive cheques and BACS receipts from customers that have previously bought from them on credit.

Activity

On 1st October TotalPhoto also received two amounts from customers in respect of their outstanding invoices. These were:

Lullabies Nursery (LUL002)   Cheque for £726.90

Mrs H Poppy   Cash £120.00

Enter these transactions onto Sage Business Cloud Accounting. Guidance follows.

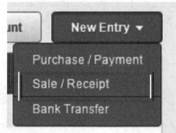

Click the   New Entry – Sale/Receipt within the 'Bank' screen.

Using the 'Customer Receipt' tab area, enter the receipt details one at a time for each payment received. These receipts will be related to a pre-existing customer invoice in the system and therefore the customer details are mandatory.

© Copyright Sage (UK) Limited 2018

✓   Type 'Lullabies Nursery' into the customer field

✓   Select Bank Account: Current

✓   Enter Receipt Date: 1st October 20XX

✓   Enter Cheque Number – *feel free to enter any 6 figure number*

The account balance (£846.90) and the related outstanding invoices will appear automatically at the bottom of the screen in the activity list.

✓   Enter the amount in the 'Amount Received' field

✓   From the activity list, select the invoices you are wishing to pay as shown

✓   Check the total amount is the amount you are wishing to pay

✓   Check 'Left to allocate' is zero

NB: It is also possible in Sage Business Cloud Accounting to receive 'payments on account'.

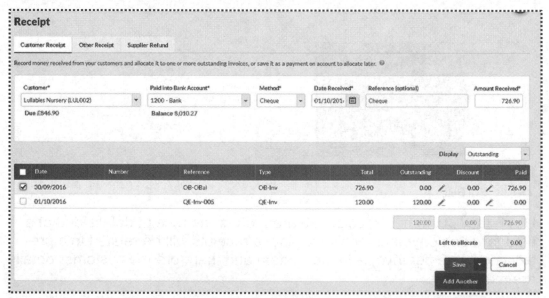

© Copyright Sage (UK) Limited 2018

Once the payment details are entered you can either 'Save' or 'Add Another'.

Now enter the second receipt, from Mrs Poppy. Note that only £120.00 has been received. This amount does not match any particular invoice, so unless notified otherwise allocate this against the oldest debt.

By clicking the 'paid' field on the line of the invoice you wish to allocate, the following screen will appear where you will be able to enter the amount received and check the outstanding balances.

Now – Click **Apply** .

Your screen should look like this:

The amount received and the allocation should have automatically updated. Now SAVE.

BACS receipts

When recording BACS receipts, you should follow the same process as when you record a cheque receipt from a customer. However, instead of entering the cheque number in the reference box, you will need to enter 'BACS' instead. The date entered should match the date that the BACS has appeared on the bank statement or the date given on the accompanying remittance advice sent by the customer.

In Sage Business Cloud Accounting it is also possible to manage sales invoices, receipts and allocations for invoices that have been created in Sage Business Cloud Accounting itself, or where there are multiple supplies (line items) in a single invoice transaction. The quick entries function will alert you if you enter the same invoice reference twice. This can be bypassed and would be acceptable if you have more than one product/supply for a particular invoice.

12 Checking bank activity

It is important for businesses to regularly check their bank transactions. There are a number of reasons for this:

- to monitor the bank balance to ensure that there is sufficient money to meet liabilities

- to monitor transactions to prevent (or identify) fraud or theft

- to ensure there is not too much money in any particular account. For example, if the balance in the current account reaches a certain level the business may decide to transfer some of it to a different account where it may earn a higher rate of interest.

In the banking tab, select the bank account you wish to check, in this case the 'Bank/Current Account' (code 1200):

Scroll down and in the date fields enter from 30th September 20XX to 30th October 20XX then click 'Search'.

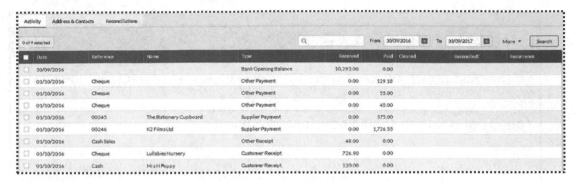

You will notice the current bank balance is now showing £8,857.17 made up of an opening balance of £10,293 with receipts of £894.90 and payments of £2330.73.

NB Sage Business Cloud Accounting supports a full 'bank reconciliation' function.

Activity

You should now produce a revised Trial Balance as at 31st October 20XX.

Your Trial Balance should now look like this.

TotalPhoto

Period Trial Balance

From: 30/09/2016	TotalPhoto		20 Jun 2018
To: 31/10/2016	Trial Balance Report		10:31

This period only

Nominal Code	Name	Selected Period	
		Debit	Credit
0030	Office equipment - Cost	4,849.00	
0031	Office equipment - Accumulated Depreciation		921.00
0032	Photographic Equipment	20,608.01	
0033	Photographic Equip Depreciation		4,316.00
0050	Motor Vehicles - Cost	21,800.00	
0051	Motor Vehicles - Accumulated Depreciation		5,450.00
1000	Stock	7,403.00	
1100	Trade Debtors	4,270.00	
1200	Bank	8,857.17	
1210	Cash in Hand	250.00	
2100	Trade Creditors		15,909.82
2200	VAT on Sales		185.30
2201	VAT on Purchases	176.35	
2202	VAT Liability		1,623.29
3100	Profit and Loss Account		5,498.28
3200	Capital introduced		20,000.00
4000	Sales - Individuals &Family		5,554.71
4001	Sales - Weddings		4,584.50
4002	Sales - Corporate		1,977.09
4003	Sales - Nurseries & Schools		11,432.20
4004	Other Sales		1,590.30

5000	Purchases - Film	414.39
5001	Purchases - Paper	1,196.87
5002	Purchases - Cartridges & Toner	1,535.15
5003	Purchases - Stationery	502.92
5004	Purchases - Other Consumables	823.52
6000	Marketing	55.00
7100	Rent & Rates	4,280.00
7340	Motor Expenses	1,035.64
7400	Travel & Entertainment	229.39
7520	Office Costs	711.08
8200	General Expenses	45.00
	TOTAL	**£79,042.49**	**£79,042.49**

13 Transfers

Sometimes a business may transfer money from one account to another. For example, it may deposit money from 'Petty Cash' to the 'Bank Current Account' or vice versa. Alternatively, it may transfer an amount from the current account to a deposit account.

 Activity

TotalPhoto currently have £250.00 in their petty cash tin and think this is too much. Therefore, they want to deposit £150.00 from the petty cash account to the bank current account. They take £150 out of the tin, then take it to the bank and pay it into the bank current account. Date the transfer 10th October 20XX.

Process this transaction onto Sage Business Cloud Accounting. Guidance follows.

When 'transferring' cash from a Cash in Hand or Petty Cash account the process in Sage Business Cloud Accounting is called a 'Bank Deposit'. All other bank account to bank account transfers are called 'Bank Transfers'.

From the banking tab, select the Cash in Hand account by clicking on the name description.

Once on the Cash in Hand Account record, using the New Entry drop down, chose 'Bank Deposit'.

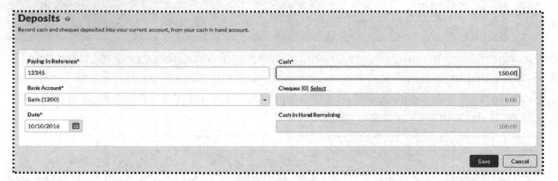

Enter a paying in slip/deposit slip reference or a meaningful reference to help you track this transaction at a later date.

Enter the bank account into which the deposit will be made. (10th Oct 20XX).

Enter £150 into the Cash field and SAVE.

The Cash in Hand account can be used to record receipts ahead of depositing a cheque into an actual bank account. This will make sure a customer account or a sales balance is correct without having to go to the bank. When the deposit is made into the bank, this can be recorded using the cheques function in the deposits screen.

14 Petty cash

Most businesses use petty cash as a way of paying for minor expenses such as taxi fares, tea, milk and coffee, window cleaning etc.

Payments out of petty cash are recorded in exactly the same way as any other payments made from a bank account. Remember to make sure that you use the correct account number (1210).

Also be sure to enter the correct VAT rate for each transaction. Many items commonly paid for out of petty cash are zero-rated, exempt or the supplier is not registered for VAT.

Use the VAT status as shown below but note that a window cleaner or taxi firm could have supplied a VAT receipt in a real business setting and, if so, this should be reflected in the entry to Sage Business Cloud Accounting.

 Activity

TotalPhoto makes the following payments out of petty cash on 10th October 20XX.

Voucher No	Description	Amount	VAT?
11762	Window cleaner	£4.00	No
11763	Tea and milk	£2.65	No
11764	Newspapers	£3.00	No
11765	Stamps	£3.60	No
11766	Pens	£1.99	Inclusive at 20.0%
11767	Taxi fare	£8.00	No
	Total for Day	**£23.24**	

Enter the above transactions onto Sage Business Cloud Accounting. Guidance follows.

From the banking tab, select the Cash in Hand account by clicking on the name description.

Once on the Cash in Hand Account record, using the New Entry drop down, chose Purchase/Payment.

From the Payment area – use the 'Other Payment' tab.

Since these payments are not being assigned to a supplier's account and are on the same date, these can be added as a single transaction with multiple lines.

It may be preferable however to post them separately if you require the voucher numbers to be displayed in other reports and list views.

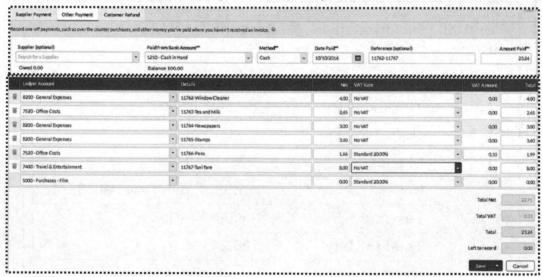

NB ensure the Amount Paid is manually entered. It will be the sum of the items entered for that day. Then SAVE. All items are entered INCLUSIVE of VAT.

The activity for the Cash in Hand account should now look like this:

Reimbursing the petty cash account

To reimburse the petty cash account, simply transfer the money from one account to the petty cash account.

Activity

TotalPhoto reimbursed their petty cash tin at the end of 13th October with the amount necessary to bring the float back to £100.00. The amount spent during the 10th October was £23.24 and so this is the amount to be reimbursed. (we didn't spend anything after 10th October). This money was taken from the 'Bank Current Account'.

Process the above transaction onto Sage Business Cloud Accounting. Guidance follows.

Step 1

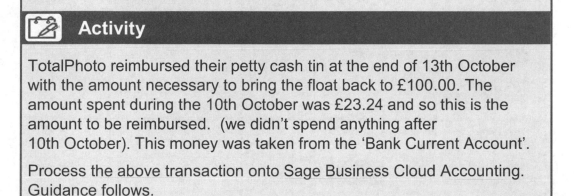

Step 2

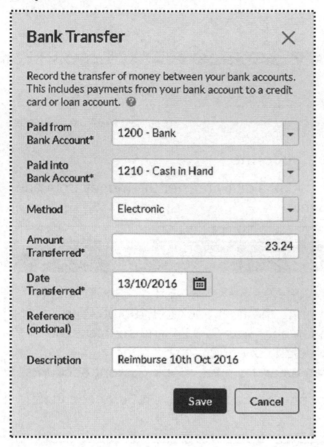

You have now learnt how to process the vast majority of transactions that most businesses will deal with on a day to day basis.

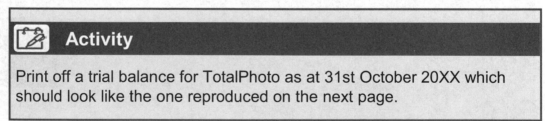

Activity

Print off a trial balance for TotalPhoto as at 31st October 20XX which should look like the one reproduced on the next page.

This one was exported to Excel:

	A	B	C	D
1	From	30/09/2016 To		31/10/2016
2	Nominal Code	Name	Selected Period	
3			Debit	Credit
4	30	Office equipment - Cost	4,843.00	
5	31	Office equipment - Accumulated Depreciation		321
6	32	Photographic Equipment	20,608.01	
7	33	Photographic Equip Depreciation		4,316.00
8	50	Motor Vehicles - Cost	21,800.00	
9	51	Motor Vehicles - Accumulated Depreciation		5,450.00
10	1000	Stock	7,403.00	
11	1100	Trade Debtors	4,270.00	
12	1200	Bank	8,983.33	
13	1210	Cash in Hand	100	
14	2100	Trade Creditors		15,909.82
15	2200	VAT on Sales		185.3
16	2201	VAT on Purchases	176.68	
17	2202	VAT Liability		1,623.29
18	3100	Profit and Loss Account		5,498.28
19	3200	Capital introduced		20,000.00
20	4000	Sales - Individuals &Family		5,554.71
21	4001	Sales - Weddings		4,584.50
22	4002	Sales - Corporate		1,977.09
23	4003	Sales - Nurseries & Schools		11,432.20
24	4004	Other Sales		1,590.30
25	5000	Purchases - Film	414.33	
26	5001	Purchases - Paper	1,136.87	
27	5002	Purchases - Cartridges & Toner	1,535.15	
28	5003	Purchases - Stationery	502.32	
29	5004	Purchases - Other Consumables	823.52	
30	6000	Marketing	55	
31	7100	Rent & Rates	4,280.00	
32	7340	Motor Expenses	1,035.64	
33	7400	Travel & Entertainment	237.39	
34	7520	Office Costs	715.39	
35	8200	General Expenses	55.6	
36		TOTAL	£73,042.43	£73,042.43

© Copyright Sage (UK) Limited 2018

Journals

9

LEARNING OBJECTIVES	CONTENTS
Process journals (4.1)	1 Introduction
Produce routine reports from the general ledger (5.2)	2 Correction of errors

1   Introduction

So far you have learnt how to process day-to-day transactions through Sage Business Cloud Accounting. These have included recording sales and purchases and making and receiving payments.

Sometimes, however, a business will need to record an accounting transaction that falls outside the 'norm'. In these instances, a **journal** is required to correct errors or make adjustments.

Common reasons for journals include:

*   correction of errors – for example, amending opening balances or removing duplicate entries

*   writing off irrecoverable debts.

    Year end adjustments such as depreciation, accruals and prepayments (you do not need to be aware of these areas for the UACS assessment as they will be covered at a higher level).

2   Correction of errors

You may find that you enter a transaction incorrectly and post it to Sage Business Cloud Accounting before you have noticed. In certain circumstances you will need to correct the error by producing a journal.

Quite often the incorrect transaction can just simply be edited, however if for example the transaction is locked – as possibly it is included as part of a reconciliation or VAT return, a compensating journal will be required.

 Activity

Earlier, you entered a payment from the bank for £55.00 to Miltonby Cricket Association for advertising in their handbook.

It has now come to light that the amount actually owed to Miltonby Cricket Association is £85 – an underpayment of £30 has been made.

You do not have time to make the additional payment of £30 ahead of a meeting where you need to present the accounts, however you want to make sure this is accounted for in the reports you are presenting.

Using a journal, reference JNL01 post a journal. The date should be 1st October 20XX. Guidance follows.

The problem – At the moment, the marketing costs are understated by £30, as we have only paid £55 instead of the correct amount of £85.

The solution – From the Journals tab, using the 'New Journal' function, open the journal screen.

Enter the details as below:

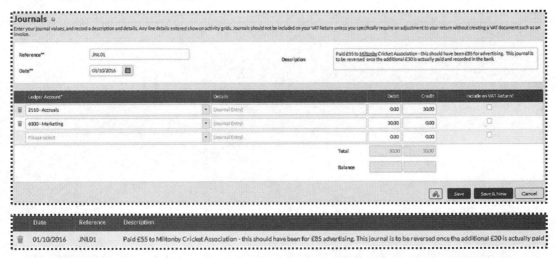

Press **Save.**

You have credited the accruals account by £30 and debited the marketing account by the same amount. When you run reports, you will notice as a result of this journal posting the marketing costs will be correct and increased by £30. Although this £30 will not as yet be reflected in the bank account the credit will however be included on the Accruals Account.

At a future date, when you have time, you can make the actual bank payment, but instead of debiting Marketing costs you will debit the Accruals Account.

Bank reconciliation

LEARNING OBJECTIVES	CONTENTS

LEARNING OBJECTIVES

Reconcile the bank statement (4.2)

Produce routine reports from the general ledger (5.2)

CONTENTS

1 Introduction

2 Performing a bank reconciliation using Sage Business Cloud Accounting

1 Introduction

A useful exercise for all businesses to undertake on a regular basis is to reconcile their bank account. In essence this means checking the company's own records with the bank statement received from their bank.

We need to review the bank reconciliation process for our case study business. TotalPhoto received the following statement from their bank.

STATEMENT No 10

15th October 20XX

Account number

Sort code

Date		Payments	Receipts	Balance
30/09/XX	Op Bal			10293.00C
01/10/XX	Counter credit		14.40	10307.40C
01/10/XX	Counter credit		33.60	10341.00C
01/10/XX	Counter credit		726.90	11067.90C
01/10/XX	Counter credit		120.00	11187.90C
01/10/XX	Interest		11.22	11199.12C
01/10/XX	Bank Charges	31.41		11167.71C
06/10/XX	DD North West Radio	240.00		10927.71C
10/10/XX	Bank Deposit		150.00	11077.71C
13/10/XX	Bank transfer	23.24		11054.47C
13/10/XX	Chq 242	55.00		10999.47C
14/10/XX	Chq 243	129.18		10870.29C
14/10/XX	Chq 244	45.00		10825.29C

D = Debit

C = Credit

The bank statement will rarely agree exactly with the company's own records, for three reasons. Let's think about what these are:

1 **Items on the bank statement not yet recorded in Sage Business Cloud Accounting**

   There may be some items on the bank statement which do not yet appear in the company's records. Here, there is interest which has been credited to the business' account of £11.22, and also bank charges of £31.41 which have been debited from the account. There is also a direct debit for £240.00. It is likely that the company would not know the exact amount or date of the first of these receipts/ payments from the bank account until the statement is actually received – further ones however can be scheduled – see recurring payments and receipts in a later chapter. You should always check however that all standing orders/direct debits/BACS transfers etc. have been fully recorded in the company's records and have been processed by the bank.

   Discrepancies between the bank statement and the company's own records of this nature should be dealt with by updating the company's records.

2 **Timing differences**

   This is a very common cause of discrepancies between the bank statement and the company's own records. Timing differences occur because the company will generally update its records before the bank has had the opportunity to process all transactions.

   Imagine the scenario where a company writes a cheque to a supplier on 1st March. The accounts clerk is likely to update the company's records (i.e. Sage Business Cloud Accounting) on that day. However, if the cheque was produced late in the afternoon it may not actually be posted until the following day and may not arrive at the supplier's address until two or three days after that. Weekends and public holidays can delay this further. It may then not be banked immediately by the supplier; it may take them two or three days to actually bank the cheque in their own branch. The cheque must then go through the banks' clearing system which may take 3–5 working days. Therefore the funds associated with that cheque (written on 1st March) may not actually be cleared out of the bank account until say 10th March or maybe later.

If a bank statement is sent to the company in this time it will not show the cheque payment, as it will not have been fully processed at the time the statement is produced. It will, however, have been recorded in the company's own accounts.

It is important therefore to undergo a process of bank reconciliation regularly to ensure that the only differences between the bank statement and the company's own records are caused by these timing differences (which can easily be accounted for), and not by the third reason for discrepancies, where an error has occurred.

3   **Errors**

It is perfectly possible for either the bank or (more likely) the company to have made an error in the course of producing their figures.

2   Performing a bank reconciliation using Sage Business Cloud Accounting

Activity

Perform a bank reconciliation for TotalPhoto using the bank statement provided at the start of this chapter. Guidance follows.

From the **Banking tab/area**, select the current account and open the bank record.

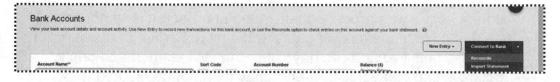

© Copyright Sage (UK) Limited 2018

Using the  function button, navigate to the Bank Reconciliation page.

(Do not use the drop down option to import the bank statement – we will manually reconcile the statement.)

Statement Date*	15/10/2016 📅		Statement End Balance*	10,825.29	Reference	Statement 10
Bank Account	Bank (1200)					Apply

Enter the Statement date 15th Oct 20XX, closing balance £10825.29 (this should be a positive figure as it is a credit on the bank statement) and

statement number 10 and **Apply**

Tip: If your account is overdrawn it would show as a debit on the bank statement, to record a negative amount enter a minus (-) at the beginning of the value. The bank statement is from the bank's perspective so an overdraft is an asset for the bank. If you are in credit, it is a liability for the bank.

Working down the bank statement, place a 'tick' in the 'Reconciled?' box at the side of the items which match, these appear on the bank activity at the bottom of the Bank Reconciliation page. The page supports 10 lines per page, it is likely there will be more than one page of transactions available for matching/reconciling.

It is useful to also manually 'tick' using a pencil any item matched on the bank statement within Sage Business Cloud Accounting.

In this example we combined the Cash Sales deposit into a single receipt of £48.00

| Other Receipt | 48.00 | 0.00 | ☑ |

Mouse –Click- Tick

Date		Payments	Receipts	Balance
30/09/16	Op Bal			✓10293.00C
01/10/16	Counter credit		✓ ⎡14.40	10307.40C
01/10/16	Counter credit		⎣33.60	10341.00C
01/10/16	Counter credit		726.90	✓11067.90C
01/10/16	Counter credit		120.00	✓11187.90C
01/10/16	Interest		11.22	11199.12C
01/10/16	Bank Charges	31.41		11167.71C
06/10/16	DD North West Radio	240.00		10927.71C
10/10/16	Bank Deposit		150.00	✓11077.71C
13/10/16	Bank transfer	23.24 ✓		11054.47C
13/10/16	Chq 242	55.00 ✓		10999.47C
14/10/16	Chq 243	129.18 ✓		10870.29C
14/10/16	Chq 244	45.00 ✓		10825.29C

The above bank statement is showing all transactions as already posted in Sage Business Cloud Accounting – indicated by a tick ✓

The following items have not been posted in Sage Business Cloud Accounting:

01/10/16	Interest		11.22	11199.12C
01/10/16	Bank Charges	31.41		11167.71C
06/10/16	DD North West Radio	240.00		10927.71C

The 'Interest and Charges' can be added directly into the Sage Business

Cloud Accounting reconciliation system using the [Interest and Charges] function.

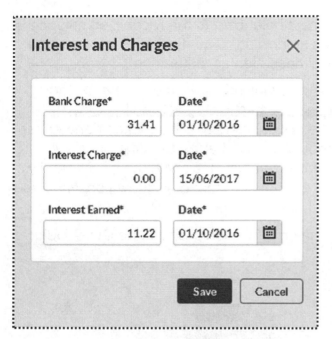

The bank charge transactions will appear at the bottom of the activity list, showing as reconciled.

This is how the reconciliation activity list should appear, depending on how it has been sorted.

Date	Reference	Name	Category	Received	Paid	Cleared	Reconciled?
30/09/2016			Bank Opening Balance	10,293.00	0.00		✓
01/10/2016	Cheque		Other Payment	0.00	129.18		✓
01/10/2016	Cheque		Other Payment	0.00	55.00		✓
01/10/2016	Cheque		Other Payment	0.00	45.00		✓
01/10/2016	00245	The Stationery Cupboard	Supplier Payment	0.00	375.00		☐
01/10/2016	00246	K2 Films Ltd	Supplier Payment	0.00	1,726.55		☐
01/10/2016	Cash Sales		Other Receipt	48.00	0.00		✓
01/10/2016	Cheque	Lullabies Nursery	Customer Receipt	726.90	0.00		✓
01/10/2016	Cash	Mrs H Poppy	Customer Receipt	120.00	0.00		✓
10/10/2016	12345		Deposit: Cash in Hand	150.00	0.00		✓
10/10/2016			Transfer: Cash in Hand	0.00	23.24		✓
01/10/2016	Bank Charge		Bank Payment	0.00	31.41		✓
01/10/2016	Interest Earned		Bank Receipt	11.22	0.00		✓

At the bottom of the screen is a reconciliation summary.

Total Received		Total Paid	
	11,349.12		283.83
Starting Balance	Target Balance*	Reconciled Balance	Difference
0.00	10,825.29	11,065.29	-240.00

The target balance is the statement balance and the reconciled balance is the sum of all bank transactions reconciled. The difference between the two is the 'unreconciled balance' described as 'difference'.

You will notice the difference is £240 which is the Direct Debit to North West Radio. This has not yet been posted in Sage Business Cloud Accounting but is included in the target balance. This can be done either after or before finalising the reconciliation – if after, the difference will be carried forward to the next reconciliation and dealt with there. Normally, to keep things less complicated it is better to make all known postings as soon as possible and not carry them forward.

Let's save the reconciliation for later so we can process the Direct Debit.

Click

From the Bank account screen go to

Enter as an 'Other Payment':

© Copyright Sage (UK) Limited 2018

Click Save then return to the Bank Reconciliation, locate the £240 transaction and tick as reconciled.

The Un-reconciled difference will now be zero.

© Copyright Sage (UK) Limited 2018

Click FINISH.

Using the print button [Print] at the top right of the screen, your reconciliation report should now look like this:

Previous reconciliations can be found in the Reconciliations tab on the bank account record screen.

TotalPhoto

TotalPhoto
Unit 63 Bailey Industrial Estate, Formby Road, Miltonby,
Lancashire, LD37 7QZ, United Kingdom

Telephone: VAT Number
01949 969 378   GB 376096823

Bank Account	Bank (1200)		Statement Date	15/10/2016
Reference	Statement 10		Reconciled By	Leanne Halsall

Date	Reference	Name	Category	Paid	Received
30/09/2016			Bank Opening Balance	0.00	10,293.00
01/10/2016	Cheque		Other Payment	129.18	0.00
01/10/2016	Cheque		Other Payment	55.00	0.00
01/10/2016	Cheque		Other Payment	45.00	0.00
01/10/2016	Cash Sales		Other Receipt	0.00	48.00
01/10/2016	Cheque	Lullabies Nursery	Customer Receipt	0.00	726.90
01/10/2016	Cash	Mrs H Poppy	Customer Receipt	0.00	120.00
10/10/2016	12345		Deposit: Cash in Hand	0.00	150.00
13/10/2016			Transfer: Cash in Hand	23.24	0.00
01/10/2016	Bank Charge		Bank Payment	31.41	0.00
01/10/2016	Interest Earned		Bank Receipt	0.00	11.22
06/10/2016	Direct Debit		Other Payment	240.00	0.00

Total Received	11,349.12
Total Paid	523.83
Starting Balance	0.00
Statement End Balance	10,825.29
Reconciled Balance	10,825.29
Difference	0.00

The purpose of a bank reconciliation is to identify:

- transactions which have been posted in the accounting system which have not appeared on the bank statement

- transactions which appear on the bank statement which have not been accounted for in the accounting system.

The sum of these items will enable you to reconcile the actual bank balance with the balance of the bank account according to the accounting system.

Following a bank reconciliation process in Sage Business Cloud Accounting, it is possible to run a report to list and total bank account postings which have not appeared on the bank statement. See Unreconciled Bank Transactions report.

The items on this report will continue to grow until a bank reconciliation process has been carried out again. When a new unreconciled bank statement is available and a new reconciliation is carried out, the available items for reconciliation/matching will be all transactions in the accounting system which have yet to be reconciled previously – per the report.

Normally all transactions which appear on the bank statement, which have not been accounted for in the accounting system, will be created and posted/matched at the time of processing the reconciliation. Very rarely there may be statement errors which need to be queried directly with the bank.

In our example, you may recall, there are two transactions in Sage Business Cloud Accounting which have yet to appear on the bank statement. These two items will be available for reconciliation when the next statement from the bank is received.

You can prove this to yourself by attempting to reconcile the next statement or running the 'Unreconciled Bank Transactions' report. Enter the last day of the financial year 30/9/20XX in the date field.

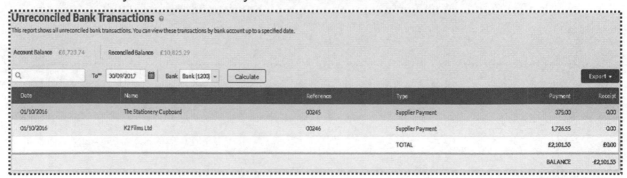

Useful reports

ASSESSMENT CRITERIA

Produce routine reports for customers and suppliers (5.1)

Produce routine reports from the general ledger (5.2)

CONTENTS

1 Introduction

2 Customer reports

3 Supplier reports

4 Bank reports

1 Introduction

There are a number of predefined reports in Sage Business Cloud Accounting, some of which you have already used. Others will be new to you. You should now make yourself familiar with these.

The reports available in Sage Business Cloud Accounting fulfil different functions, statutory (VAT) and operational through to management reports. Have a go at generating these reports using the Reporting tab or using the reports available in the module areas using the 'More' function button.

In order to select the data you wish to view in the report use the 'Period' field. To select dates you need to select 'custom'

© Copyright Sage (UK) Limited 2018

Ensure you are comfortable with the different output options, i.e. PDF and CSV or on-screen views. Practice saving the file as a PDF. This will be required as part of your assessment so it's an essential part of your studies.

You can practice as much as you like in order to familiarise yourself with the process.

Reporting Menu:

© Copyright Sage (UK) Limited 2018

Example of reports available from module areas:

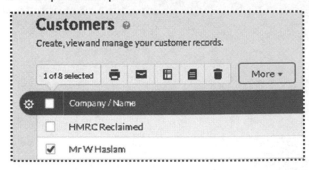

© Copyright Sage (UK) Limited 2018

Some reports will display immediately, however certain reports will be generated and accessed from the navigation bar at the top of the screen:

You also have the option with certain reports to select 'summary' or 'detailed'.

2 Customer reports

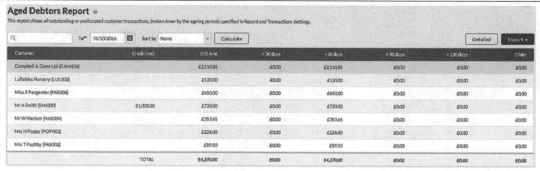

Shows a list of debtors with analysis of how long the debts have been in existence.

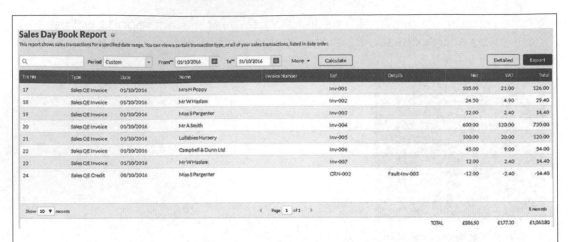

Sales Day Book Report

This report shows sales transactions for a specified date range. You can view a certain transaction type, or all of your sales transactions, listed in date order.

Trx No	Type	Date	Name	Invoice Number	Ref	Details	Net	VAT	Total
17	Sales QE Invoice	01/10/2016	Mrs H Poppy		Inv-001		105.00	21.00	126.00
18	Sales QE Invoice	01/10/2016	Mr W Haslam		Inv-002		24.50	4.90	29.40
19	Sales QE Invoice	01/10/2016	Miss S Pargenter		Inv-003		12.00	2.40	14.40
20	Sales QE Invoice	01/10/2016	Mr A Smith		Inv-004		600.00	120.00	720.00
21	Sales QE Invoice	01/10/2016	Lullabies Nursery		Inv-005		100.00	20.00	120.00
22	Sales QE Invoice	01/10/2016	Campbell & Dunn Ltd		Inv-006		45.00	9.00	54.00
23	Sales QE Invoice	01/10/2016	Mr W Haslam		Inv-007		12.00	2.40	14.40
24	Sales QE Credit	08/10/2016	Miss S Pargenter		CRN-002	Fault-Inv-003	-12.00	-2.40	-14.40

Show 10 records   Page 1 of 1   8 records

			TOTAL	£886.50	£177.30	£1,063.80

Shows a list of all invoices and credit notes produced including the Net, VAT and Gross Amounts.

Customer Activity (Accessed from Customer List)

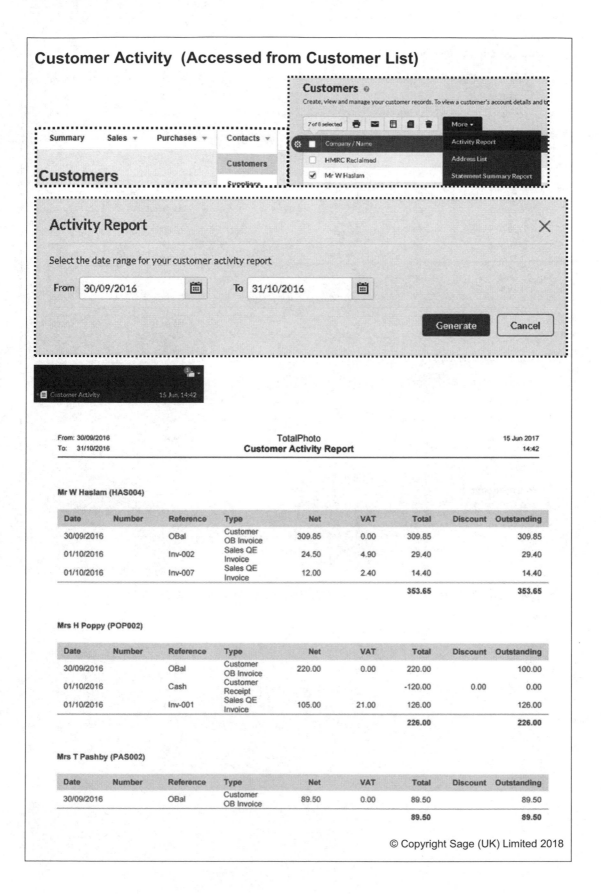

Campbell & Dunn Ltd (CAM004)

Date	Number	Reference	Type	Net	VAT	Total	Discount	Outstanding
30/09/2016		OBal	Customer OB Invoice	2,056.85	0.00	2,056.85		2,056.85
01/10/2016		Inv-006	Sales QE Invoice	45.00	9.00	54.00		54.00
						2,110.85		2,110.85

Lullabies Nursery (LUL002)

Date	Number	Reference	Type	Net	VAT	Total	Discount	Outstanding
30/09/2016		OBal	Customer OB Invoice	726.90	0.00	726.90		0.00
01/10/2016		Cheque	Customer Receipt			-726.90	0.00	0.00
01/10/2016		Inv-005	Sales QE Invoice	100.00	20.00	120.00		120.00

From: 30/09/2016	TotalPhoto	15 Jun 2017
To: 31/10/2016	**Customer Activity Report**	14:42

						120.00		120.00

Miss S Pargenter (PAR006)

Date	Number	Reference	Type	Net	VAT	Total	Discount	Outstanding
30/09/2016		OBal	Customer OB Invoice	650.00	0.00	650.00		650.00
01/10/2016		Inv-003	Sales QE Invoice	12.00	2.40	14.40		0.00
08/10/2016		CRN-002	Sales QE Credit	-12.00	-2.40	-14.40		0.00
						650.00		650.00

Mr A Smith (SMI009)

Date	Number	Reference	Type	Net	VAT	Total	Discount	Outstanding
01/10/2016		Inv-004	Sales QE Invoice	600.00	120.00	720.00		720.00
						720.00		720.00

Shows all transactions for customers (i.e. sales and receipts)

| | TotalPhoto | | | | 15 Jun 2017 |
| | **Customer Address List** | | | | 14:46 |

Address Types: All

Customer Name	Address	Contact name	Phone	Mobile	Email	Fax
Mr W Haslam (HAS004)	22 Brown Street Miltonby Lancashire LN87 6FD	Main Contact				
Mrs H Poppy (POP002)	120 Forrest Way Miltonby Lancashire LN87 9YR	Main Contact				
Mrs T Pashby (PAS002)	3GA Andrews Street Killington Lancashire LN85 6TT	Main Contact				
Campbell & Dunn Ltd (CAM004)	12 The Beeches Miltonby Lancashire LN87 9PP	Main Contact				
Lullabies Nursery (LUL002)	104 Victoria Road Miltonby Lancashire LN87 5PS	Main Contact				
Miss S Pargenter (PAR006)	11 Alexandra Park Miltonby Lancashire LN87 2WD	Main Contact				
Mr A Smith (SMI009)	12 Main Street Miltonby Lancashire LN87 4DF	Main Contact				

Shows address details, contact name etc. for customers

3 Supplier reports

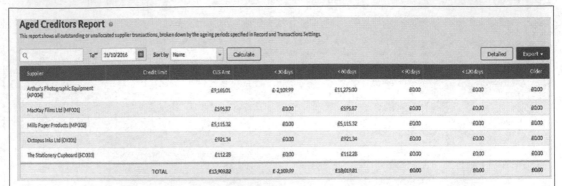

Aged Creditors Report

This report shows all outstanding or unallocated supplier transactions, broken down by the ageing periods specified in Record and Transactions Settings.

To: 31/10/2016 Sort by: Name Calculate Detailed Export ▾

Supplier	Credit limit	O/S Amt	< 30 days	< 60 days	< 90 days	< 120 days	Older
Arthur's Photographic Equipment (AP004)		£9,165.01	£-2,109.99	£11,275.00	£0.00	£0.00	£0.00
Mackay Films Ltd (MF001)		£595.87	£0.00	£595.87	£0.00	£0.00	£0.00
Mills Paper Products (MP002)		£5,115.32	£0.00	£5,115.32	£0.00	£0.00	£0.00
Octopus Inks Ltd (OI001)		£921.34	£0.00	£921.34	£0.00	£0.00	£0.00
The Stationery Cupboard (SC003)		£112.28	£0.00	£112.28	£0.00	£0.00	£0.00
	TOTAL	£15,909.82	£-2,109.99	£18,019.81	£0.00	£0.00	£0.00

© Copyright Sage (UK) Limited 2018

Shows the outstanding creditor balances and the how long the debts have been in existence. The aging will be dynamic based on the 'To Date' i.e. retrospective aging calculation.

From: 30/09/2016
To: 31/10/2016

TotalPhoto
Supplier Activity Report

15 Jun 2017
14:49

Mackay Films Ltd (MF001)

Date	Number	Reference	Type	Net	VAT	Total	Discount	Outstanding
30/09/2016		OBal	Supplier OB Invoice	345.36	0.00	345.36		345.36
01/10/2016		Inv 1341	Purchase QE Invoice	208.76	41.75	250.51		250.51
						595.87		595.87

K2 Films Ltd (KF001)

Date	Number	Reference	Type	Net	VAT	Total	Discount	Outstanding
30/09/2016		OBal	Supplier OB Invoice	1,726.55	0.00	1,726.55		0.00
01/10/2016		00246	Supplier Payment			-1,726.55	0.00	0.00
						0.00		0.00

The Stationery Cupboard (SC003)

Date	Number	Reference	Type	Net	VAT	Total	Discount	Outstanding
30/09/2016		OBal	Supplier OB Invoice	375.00	0.00	375.00		0.00
01/10/2016		Inv 209	Purchase QE Invoice	14.65	2.93	17.58		17.58
01/10/2016		Inv 216	Purchase QE Invoice	78.92	15.78	94.70		94.70
01/10/2016		00245	Supplier Payment			-375.00	0.00	0.00
						112.28		112.28

© Copyright Sage (UK) Limited 2018

Mills Paper Products (MP002)

Date	Number	Reference	Type	Net	VAT	Total	Discount	Outstanding
30/09/2016		OBal	Supplier OB Invoice	4,920.30	0.00	4,920.30		4,920.30
01/10/2016		Inv 10092	Purchase QE Invoice	162.52	32.50	195.02		195.02
						5,115.32		**5,115.32**

Octopus Inks Ltd (OI001)

Date	Number	Reference	Type	Net	VAT	Total	Discount	Outstanding
30/09/2016		OBal	Supplier OB Invoice	550.20	0.00	550.20		550.20
01/10/2016		Inv 2203	Purchase QE Invoice	309.28	61.86	371.14		371.14

Who: Leanne Halsall	Produced by Sage One	Page 1 of 2

From: 30/09/2016	TotalPhoto	15 Jun 2017
To: 31/10/2016	**Supplier Activity Report**	14:49

	921.34	921.34

Arthur's Photographic Equipment Ltd (AP004)

Date	Number	Reference	Type	Net	VAT	Total	Discount	Outstanding
30/09/2016		OBal	Supplier OB Invoice	11,275.00	0.00	11,275.00		11,275.00
08/10/2016		134C	Purchase QE Credit	-2,109.99	0.00	-2,109.99		-2,109.99
						9,165.01		**9,165.01**

Shows all transactions for a single, or range of, suppliers, including purchases, returns, payments etc.

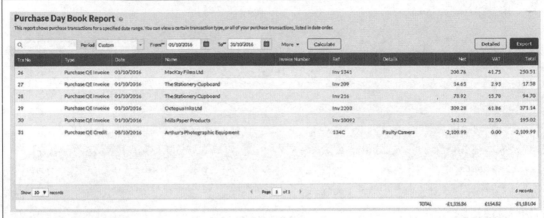

© Copyright Sage (UK) Limited 2018

Shows the list of all invoices and credit notes received.

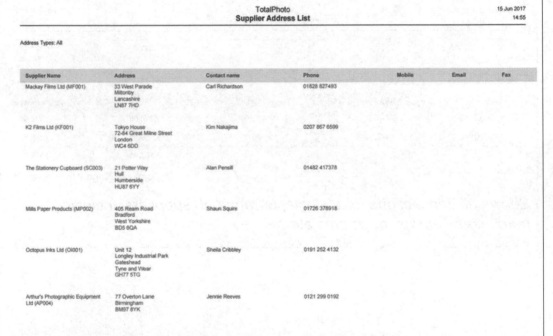

Shows address details, contact name etc. for suppliers

© Copyright Sage (UK) Limited 2018

KAPLAN PUBLISHING

4 Bank reports

TotalPhoto

TotalPhoto
Unit 63 Bailey Industrial Estate, Fornby Road, Miltonby,
Lancashire, LD37 7QZ, United Kingdom

Telephone: **VAT Number**
01949 969 378   GB 376096823

| Bank Account | Bank (1200) | | | Statement Date | 15/10/2016 |
| Reference | Statement 10 | | | Reconciled By | Leanne Halsall |

Date	Reference	Name	Category	Paid	Received
30/09/2016			Bank Opening Balance	0.00	10,293.00
01/10/2016	Cheque		Other Payment	129.18	0.00
01/10/2016	Cheque		Other Payment	55.00	0.00
01/10/2016	Cheque		Other Payment	45.00	0.00
01/10/2016	Cash Sales		Other Receipt	0.00	48.00
01/10/2016	Cheque	Lullabies Nursery	Customer Receipt	0.00	726.90
01/10/2016	Cash	Mrs H Poppy	Customer Receipt	0.00	120.00
10/10/2016	12345		Deposit: Cash in Hand	0.00	150.00
13/10/2016			Transfer: Cash in Hand	23.24	0.00
01/10/2016	Bank Charge		Bank Payment	31.41	0.00
01/10/2016	Interest Earned		Bank Receipt	0.00	11.22
06/10/2016	Direct Debit		Other Payment	240.00	0.00

Total Received	11,349.12
Total Paid	523.83
Starting Balance	0.00
Statement End Balance	10,825.29
Reconciled Balance	10,825.29
Difference	0.00

Shows all bank transactions that have been successfully matched and reconciled to the bank statement

The above report can be accessed by going to the bank module, click on the current account then scroll down the page and near activity click 'reconciliations' tab. Click on the statement reconciliation you would like to view. You may then click 'print' at the top right to view the bank transactions that have been successfully reconciled for your recent bank statement.

Recurring entries

12

ASSESSMENT CRITERIA	CONTENTS

ASSESSMENT CRITERIA

Process recurring receipts and payments (3.2)

CONTENTS

1   Introduction

2   Creating a new recurring payment

3   Recurring receipts

1 Introduction

A company often pays and receives money on a regular basis. For example, it may pay bills monthly or quarterly to organisations for payment such as insurance or rates. Also, it may receive money regularly from customers or other parties, for example receipts for rental income. To make life easier, Sage Business Cloud Accounting allows regular payments and receipts to be entered, automatically, as a 'recurring entry'.

2 Creating a new recurring payment

How to process a recurring entry

Recurring payments and receipts are created from pre-existing transactions.

From the Banking tab, select the Current Account by clicking on it.

From within the 'Activity' tab inside the bank account record screen, locate the £240 direct debit payment for marketing from North West Radio.

This can be done simply using the date and/or 'transaction type' filters. In this example a combination of dates and search text 'direct debit' was used.

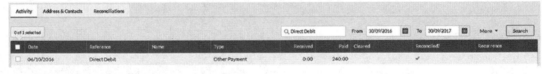

© Copyright Sage (UK) Limited 2018

Select the payment transaction by clicking on it.

You will notice this item has been included in a bank reconciliation – it was identified during the bank reconciliation process.

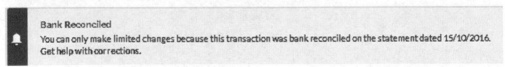

© Copyright Sage (UK) Limited 2018

A new button will be displaying on the payment transaction record.

Make Recurring

Using the 'Make Recurring' option, set up as follows:

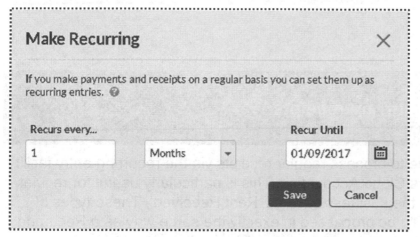

© Copyright Sage (UK) Limited 2018

This set up means the payment will recur once a month until a date set in the future. Click SAVE.

The number of recurrences is determined by the numerical value you enter and the frequency you choose, i.e. weekly, monthly etc.

When you now view the bank activity change the 'To' date so it is equal to '01/09/2017' and you will notice the recurring transactions have been entered automatically up until either today or to the Recur until date. Sage Business Cloud Accounting is cloud based so 'todays' date will always be the current date.

© Copyright Sage (UK) Limited 2018

The [icon] symbol will appear against the last recurring transaction. If you wish to extend or stop the recurring period, select this item from the

activity list and [**Edit Recurring**] then you may edit or click

[**Stop recurrence**]

3 Recurring receipts

You are also able to process regular receipts via the recurring entry facility in Sage Business Cloud Accounting. This is particularly useful for regular amounts sent to the business such as 'Rent Received'. These types of transactions would be processed in exactly the same way as a Recurring Payment, except the transaction type will be based on a previously created 'Other Receipt'.

Amending company details and managing data

13

KNOWLEDGE

There are no relevant 'learning outcomes' applicable to this section of the workbook, as the topics covered are not part of the assessment process. However, you are recommended to fully familiarise yourself with all aspects of this chapter.

CONTENTS

1   Amending data
2   Resetting data

1   Amending data

As we have already seen, one way to correct an error is by means of a journal. This is essentially a book-keeping solution, using a double entry to correct or amend an earlier error. In Sage Business Cloud Accounting we need to use a journal when the incorrect transaction is included in a reconciliation, VAT return or allocation. Reconciliations can, however, be reversed to allow amendment – make the amendment directly before reprocessing the allocation or reconciliation.

2   Resetting Data

When you are practising on Sage Business Cloud Accounting, you may need to 'reset' data and start again from scratch. For example, this could be required if you have made significant errors or wish to work through a brand new scenario.

Resetting will remove all of the transactions and accounts set up data that have previously been entered, including any additional nominal codes, suppliers and customers etc. As previously explained, you are unable to change the business name. The set-up instructions are featured at the beginning of the text book in chapter 3. These should be followed again when you are ready to start a new scenario.

Despite the severe implications of a data reset, it is a relatively straightforward process to follow:

Click the small drop down arrow next to the business name 'TotalPhoto' on the black navigation bar at the top right of the screen, select 'Manage Business Account'.

© Copyright Sage (UK) Limited 2018

Select:

and then

Enter your email address, then 'Reset Data'.

Once the data is cleared, click on the word 'Accounting' on the top left and you will be taken back to the set-up process.

The business name will be Kaplan Financial. You are unable to change this name for your studies.

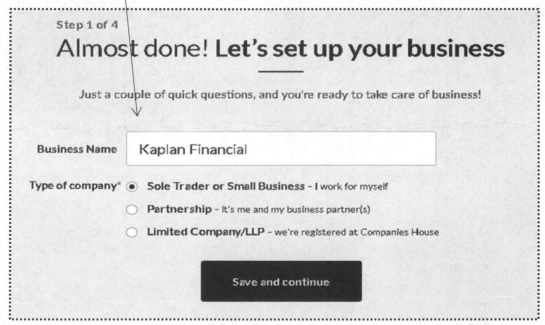

This functionality is for use in your studies. You would be unlikely to use it in the workplace.

Creating a password to protect data

KNOWLEDGE
There are no relevant 'learning outcomes' applicable to this section of the workbook, as the topics covered are not part of the assessment process for AQ2016. However, you are recommended to fully familiarise yourself with all aspects of this chapter.

CONTENTS
1   Changing a password to protect data

1 Changing a password to protect data

It is important to protect your accounting data with the sufficient level of security. Sage Business Cloud Accounting is a highly secure on-line platform, however it is up to you to make sure your password is not easily guessed by someone who may know some information about you. Your authentication provider including SageID will however ensure the length and content of the passwords and the types of security questions are of sufficient structure.

Depending how you have signed in to Sage Business Cloud Accounting, will determine how you are authenticated and where you set up and manage your password.

If you have signed up with a SageID you will be able to manage your password and security directly from within Sage Business Cloud Accounting itself.

SageID: How to change your password

If you need to change your password, from the black navigation bar at the top right of the screen click the business name then 'Manage Business Account,

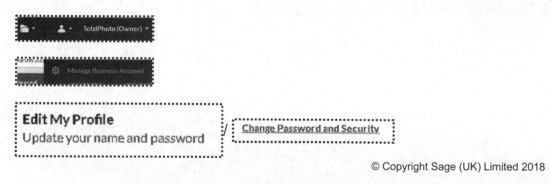

You are able to change your password and/or your security settings. Your existing password and questions will be required in order to make changes.

Follow the instructions on the screen.

2 Practice assessment answers

Task 3.4 Customer Address List

Task 3.4 Supplier Address List

Task 3.4 Trial Balance

From: 31/01/2016
To: 01/01/2017

Justin Timbercrafts
Trial Balance Report

26 Jun 2017
10:25

This period only

Nominal Code	Name	Selected Period	
		Debit	Credit
0030	IT Equipment	3,684.00	
0050	Motor Vehicles - Cost	4,586.00	
1100	Trade Debtors	14,978.95	
1200	Bank Current	10,203.30	
1210	Petty Cash	150.00	
1220	Bank Deposit	1,000.00	
2100	Trade Creditors		7,432.51
3200	Capital		20,000.00
4000	Sales - Jungle Collection		17,293.50
4001	Sales - Farm Collection		19,224.70
4002	Sales - Pets Collection		10,260.45
4003	Cash Sales		5,431.40
5000	Cost of sales - Materials	28,344.80	
6200	Marketing	1,420.00	
7100	Rent and rates	2,400.00	
7300	Motor Expenses	9,805.51	
7500	Office costs	2,350.00	
7610	Insurance	720.00	
	TOTAL	£79,642.56	£79,642.56

Task 12 New Customer Record

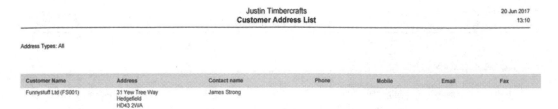

Task 18 Recurring entry screen shots

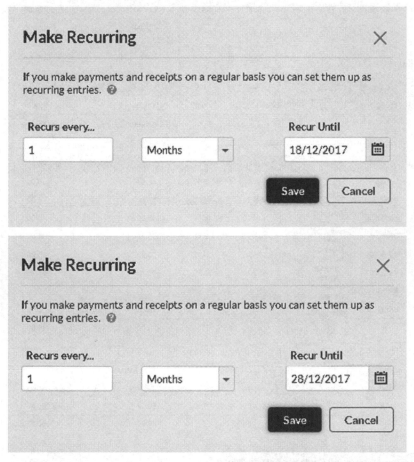

Task 23 Customer Activity Report

From: 31/12/2016
To: 31/01/2017

Justin Timbercrafts
Customer Activity Report

20 Jun 2017
15:49

Toyways plc (TW003)

Date	Number	Reference	Type	Net	VAT	Total	Discount	Outstanding
31/12/2016		Inv 00288	Customer OB Invoice	1,235.76	0.00	1,235.76		0.00
02/01/2017		Inv 00301	Sales QE Invoice	35.00	7.00	42.00		42.00
02/01/2017		Inv 00301	Sales QE Invoice	45.00	9.00	54.00		54.00
02/01/2017		Inv 00301	Sales QE Invoice	45.00	9.00	54.00		54.00
03/01/2017		Cheque	Customer Receipt			-1,235.76	0.00	0.00
06/01/2017		Inv 00304	Sales QE Invoice	270.00	54.00	324.00		324.00
						474.00		**474.00**

Perfect Pastimes Ltd (PP002)

Date	Number	Reference	Type	Net	VAT	Total	Discount	Outstanding
31/12/2016		Inv 00291	Customer OB Invoice	13,209.34	0.00	13,209.34		13,209.34
						13,209.34		**13,209.34**

Happykidz Ltd (HK006)

Date	Number	Reference	Type	Net	VAT	Total	Discount	Outstanding
31/12/2016		Inv 00299	Customer OB Invoice	342.98	0.00	342.98		0.00
02/01/2017		Inv 00300	Sales QE Invoice	56.00	11.20	67.20		0.00
02/01/2017		Inv 00300	Sales QE Invoice	90.00	18.00	108.00		0.00
02/01/2017		CRN 55	Sales QE Credit	-14.00	-2.80	-16.80		0.00
04/01/2017		Inv 00302	Sales QE Invoice	28.00	5.60	33.60		33.60
04/01/2017		Inv 00302	Sales QE Invoice	72.00	14.40	86.40		86.40
05/01/2017		BACS	Customer Receipt			-342.98	0.00	0.00
11/01/2017		BACS	Customer Receipt			-158.40	0.00	0.00
						120.00		**120.00**

Prettypops Ltd (PP004)

Date	Number	Reference	Type	Net	VAT	Total	Discount	Outstanding
31/12/2016		Inv 00212	Customer OB Invoice	190.87	0.00	190.87		190.87
						190.87		**190.87**

From: 31/12/2016
To: 31/01/2017

Justin Timbercrafts
Customer Activity Report

20 Jun 2017
15:49

Funnystuff Ltd (FS001)

Date	Number	Reference	Type	Net	VAT	Total	Discount	Outstanding
06/01/2017		Inv 00303	Sales QE Invoice	35.00	7.00	42.00		42.00
06/01/2017		Inv 00303	Sales QE Invoice	45.00	9.00	54.00		54.00
						96.00		**96.00**

Task 23 Supplier Activity Report

| From: 31/12/2016 | | Justin Timbercrafts | | | | | | 20 Jun 2017 |
| To: 31/01/2017 | | Supplier Activity Report | | | | | | 15:56 |

Matchsticks Ltd (MCS003)

Date	Number	Reference	Type	Net	VAT	Total	Discount	Outstanding
31/12/2016		Inv 2033	Supplier OB Invoice	1,943.26	0.00	1,943.26		0.00
04/01/2017		0012672	Supplier Payment			-1,943.26	0.00	0.00
08/01/2017		Inv 3178	Purchase QE Invoice	1,400.00	280.00	1,680.00		1,680.00
						1,680.00		1,680.00

Willow Works Ltd (WWW002)

Date	Number	Reference	Type	Net	VAT	Total	Discount	Outstanding
31/12/2016		Inv 38842	Supplier OB Invoice	288.29	0.00	288.29		0.00
06/01/2017		Inv 99128	Purchase QE Invoice	240.00	48.00	288.00		288.00
11/01/2017		0012674	Supplier Payment			-288.29	0.00	0.00
						288.00		288.00

Grange Toys Ltd (GRT005)

Date	Number	Reference	Type	Net	VAT	Total	Discount	Outstanding
31/12/2016		Inv GT2640	Supplier OB Invoice	4,277.50	0.00	4,277.50		1,277.50
03/01/2017		Inv GT2882	Purchase QE Invoice	1,060.00	212.00	1,272.00		1,272.00
11/01/2017		Inv GT2916	Purchase QE Invoice	560.00	112.00	672.00		672.00
14/01/2017		0012675	Supplier Payment			-3,000.00	0.00	0.00
						3,221.50		3,221.50

FLW Ltd (FLW002)

Date	Number	Reference	Type	Net	VAT	Total	Discount	Outstanding
31/12/2016		Inv 2727	Supplier OB Invoice	923.46	0.00	923.46		0.00
04/01/2017		0012671	Supplier Payment			-923.46	0.00	0.00
						0.00		0.00

Dornley Evening Chronicle (DEC004)

Date	Number	Reference	Type	Net	VAT	Total	Discount	Outstanding
02/01/2017		Inv 2929/11	Purchase QE Invoice	130.00	26.00	156.00		0.00

| From: 31/12/2016 | | Justin Timbercrafts | | | | | | 20 Jun 2017 |
| To: 31/01/2017 | | Supplier Activity Report | | | | | | 15:56 |

Date	Number	Reference	Type	Net	VAT	Total	Discount	Outstanding
14/01/2017		0012676	Supplier Payment			-156.00	0.00	0.00
						0.00		0.00

Task 23 Trial Balance as 31st January

| From: 30/12/2016
To: 31/01/2017 | Justin Timbercrafts
Trial Balance Report | | 20 Jun 2017
16:09 |

This period only

Nominal Code	Name	Selected Period	
		Debit	Credit
0030	IT Equipment	3,892.33	
0050	Motor Vehicles - Cost	4,586.00	
1100	Trade Debtors	14,090.21	
1200	Bank Current	14,713.97	
1210	Petty Cash	150.00	
1220	Bank Deposit	1,000.00	
1230	Bank Loan		10,000.00
2100	Trade Creditors		5,189.50
2200	VAT on Sales		171.49
2201	VAT on Purchases	729.54	
3200	Capital		20,000.00
3260	Drawings	200.00	
4000	Sales - Jungle Collection		17,428.50
4001	Sales - Farm Collection		19,364.70
4002	Sales - Pets Collection		10,692.45
4003	Cash Sales		5,581.85
5000	Cost of sales - Materials	31,604.80	
6200	Marketing	1,550.00	
7100	Rent and rates	2,920.00	
7300	Motor Expenses	9,805.51	
7400	Travel and Entertainment	14.80	
7500	Office costs	2,419.33	
7610	Insurance	870.00	
7800	Repairs and renewals		150.00
7900	Bank charges and interest	32.00	
	TOTAL	£88,578.49	£88,578.49

Task 23 Audit Trail for January

| From: 31/12/2016 | | | | Justin Timbercrafts | | | | | | | | | 20 Jun 2017 |
| To: 31/01/2017 | | | | **Audit Trail Breakdown** | | | | | | | | | 16:12 |

Type: All, Status: All

Trx No	Entry Date	User	Trx Date	Name	Type	Invoice Number	Ref	Ledger Account	Debit	Credit	Deleted	VAT Reconciled	Bank Reconciled	Created By
1	20/06/2017	LH	31/12/2016	Toyways plc (TW003)	Customer OB Invoice		Inv 00288	Opening Balances Control Account (9998)		1,235.76	No	No	No	Leanne Halsall
								Trade Debtors (1100)	1,235.76			No	No	
2	20/06/2017	LH	31/12/2016	Perfect Pastimes Ltd (PP002)	Customer OB Invoice		Inv 00291	Opening Balances Control Account (9998)		13,209.34	No	No	No	Leanne Halsall
								Trade Debtors (1100)	13,209.34			No	No	
3	20/06/2017	LH	31/12/2016	Happykidz Ltd (HK006)	Customer OB Invoice		Inv 00299	Opening Balances Control Account (9998)		342.98	No	No	No	Leanne Halsall
								Trade Debtors (1100)	342.98			No	No	
4	20/06/2017	LH	31/12/2016	Prettypops Ltd (PP004)	Customer OB Invoice		Inv 00212	Opening Balances Control Account (9998)		190.87	No	No	No	Leanne Halsall
								Trade Debtors (1100)	190.87			No	No	
5	20/06/2017	LH	31/12/2016	Matchsticks Ltd (MCS003)	Supplier OB Invoice		Inv 2033	Trade Creditors (2100)		1,943.26	No	No	No	Leanne Halsall
								Opening Balances Control Account (9998)	1,943.26			No	No	
6	20/06/2017	LH	31/12/2016	Willow Works Ltd (WWW002)	Supplier OB Invoice		Inv 38842	Trade Creditors (2100)		288.29	No	No	No	Leanne Halsall
								Opening Balances Control Account (9998)	288.29			No	No	
7	20/06/2017	LH	31/12/2016	Grange Toys Ltd (GRT005)	Supplier OB Invoice		Inv GT2640	Trade Creditors (2100)		4,277.50	No	No	No	Leanne Halsall
								Opening Balances Control Account (9998)	4,277.50			No	No	
8	20/06/2017	LH	31/12/2016	FLW Ltd (FLW002)	Supplier OB Invoice		Inv 2727	Trade Creditors (2100)		923.46	No	No	No	Leanne Halsall
								Opening Balances Control Account (9998)	923.46			No	No	
9	20/06/2017	LH	31/12/2016		Bank Opening Balance			Opening Balances Control Account (9998)		11,203.30	No	No	No	Leanne Halsall

| From: 31/12/2016 | | | | Justin Timbercrafts | | | | | | | | | 20 Jun 2017 |
| To: 31/01/2017 | | | | **Audit Trail Breakdown** | | | | | | | | | 16:12 |

Trx No	Entry Date	User	Trx Date	Name	Type	Invoice Number	Ref	Ledger Account	Debit	Credit	Deleted	VAT Reconciled	Bank Reconciled	Created By
								Bank Current (1200)	11,203.30			No	Yes	
10	20/06/2017	LH	31/12/2016		Bank Opening Balance			Opening Balances Control Account (9998)		150.00	No	No	No	Leanne Halsall
								Petty Cash (1210)	150.00			No	No	
11	20/06/2017	LH	31/12/2016		Journal Opening Balance		OBals 31/12/16	Motor Vehicles - Cost (0050)	4,586.00		No	No	No	Leanne Halsall
								Opening Balances Control Account (9998)		4,586.00		No	No	
								IT Equipment (0030)	3,684.00			No	No	
								Opening Balances Control Account (9998)		3,684.00		No	No	
								Sales - Jungle Collection (4000)		17,293.50		No	No	
								Opening Balances Control Account (9998)	17,293.50			No	No	
								Sales - Farm Collection (4001)		19,224.70		No	No	
								Opening Balances Control Account (9998)	19,224.70			No	No	
								Sales - Pets Collection (4002)		10,260.45		No	No	
								Opening Balances Control Account (9998)	10,260.45			No	No	
								Cash Sales (4003)		5,431.40		No	No	
								Opening Balances Control Account (9998)	5,431.40			No	No	
								Capital (3200)		20,000.00		No	No	
								Opening Balances Control Account (9998)	20,000.00			No	No	
								Rent and rates (7100)	2,400.00			No	No	
								Opening Balances Control Account (9998)		2,400.00		No	No	
								Insurance (7610)	720.00			No	No	

Justin Timbercrafts
Audit Trail Breakdown

							Account						
							Opening Balances Control Account (9998)		720.00		No	No	
							Marketing (6200)	1,420.00			No	No	
							Opening Balances Control Account (9998)		1,420.00		No	No	
							Cost of sales - Materials (5000)	28,344.80			No	No	
							Opening Balances Control Account (9998)		28,344.80		No	No	
							Office costs (7500)	2,350.00			No	No	
							Opening Balances Control Account (9998)		2,350.00		No	No	
							Motor Expenses (7300)	9,805.51			No	No	
							Opening Balances Control Account (9998)		9,805.51		No	No	
12	20/06/2017	LH	01/01/2017		Bank Transfer	TRF01	Bank Current (1200)		1,000.00	No	No	Yes	Leanne Halsall
							Bank Deposit (1220)	1,000.00			No	No	
13	20/06/2017	LH	02/01/2017	Happykidz Ltd (HK006)	Sales QE Invoice	Inv 00300	Sales - Farm Collection (4001)		56.00	No	No	No	Leanne Halsall
							VAT on Sales (2200)		11.20		No	No	
							Trade Debtors (1100)	67.20			No	No	
14	20/06/2017	LH	02/01/2017	Happykidz Ltd (HK006)	Sales QE Invoice	Inv 00300	Sales - Jungle Collection (4000)		90.00	No	No	No	Leanne Halsall
							VAT on Sales (2200)		18.00		No	No	
							Trade Debtors (1100)	108.00			No	No	
15	20/06/2017	LH	02/01/2017	Toyways plc (TW003)	Sales QE Invoice	Inv 00301	Sales - Farm Collection (4001)		35.00	No	No	No	Leanne Halsall
							VAT on Sales (2200)		7.00		No	No	
							Trade Debtors (1100)	42.00			No	No	
16	20/06/2017	LH	02/01/2017	Toyways plc (TW003)	Sales QE Invoice	Inv 00301	Sales - Jungle Collection (4000)		45.00	No	No	No	Leanne Halsall
							VAT on Sales (2200)		9.00		No	No	
							Trade Debtors (1100)	54.00			No	No	

Justin Timbercrafts
Audit Trail Breakdown

							Account						
17	20/06/2017	LH	02/01/2017	Toyways plc (TW003)	Sales QE Invoice	Inv 00301	Sales - Pets Collection (4002)		45.00	No	No	No	Leanne Halsall
							VAT on Sales (2200)		9.00		No	No	
							Trade Debtors (1100)	54.00			No	No	
18	20/06/2017	LH	04/01/2017	Happykidz Ltd (HK006)	Sales QE Invoice	Inv 00302	Sales - Farm Collection (4001)		28.00	No	No	No	Leanne Halsall
							VAT on Sales (2200)		5.60		No	No	
							Trade Debtors (1100)	33.60			No	No	
19	20/06/2017	LH	04/01/2017	Happykidz Ltd (HK006)	Sales QE Invoice	Inv 00302	Sales - Pets Collection (4002)		72.00	No	No	No	Leanne Halsall
							VAT on Sales (2200)		14.40		No	No	
							Trade Debtors (1100)	86.40			No	No	
20	20/06/2017	LH	02/01/2017	Happykidz Ltd (HK006)	Sales QE Credit	CRN 55	Trade Debtors (1100)		16.80	No	No	No	Leanne Halsall
							Sales - Farm Collection (4001)	14.00			No	No	
							VAT on Sales (2200)	2.80			No	No	
21	20/06/2017	LH	02/01/2017	Domley Evening Chronicle (DEC004)	Purchase QE Invoice	Inv 2929/11	Trade Creditors (2100)		156.00	No	No	No	Leanne Halsall
							Marketing (6200)	130.00			No	No	
							VAT on Purchases (2201)	26.00			No	No	
22	20/06/2017	LH	03/01/2017	Grange Toys Ltd (GRT005)	Purchase QE Invoice	Inv GT2882	Trade Creditors (2100)		1,272.00	No	No	No	Leanne Halsall
							Cost of sales - Materials (5000)	1,060.00			No	No	
							VAT on Purchases (2201)	212.00			No	No	
23	20/06/2017	LH	06/01/2017	Willow Works Ltd (WWW002)	Purchase QE Invoice	Inv 99128	Trade Creditors (2100)		288.00	No	No	No	Leanne Halsall
							Cost of sales - Materials (5000)	240.00			No	No	
							VAT on Purchases (2201)	48.00			No	No	
24	20/06/2017	LH	03/01/2017	Toyways plc (TW003)	Customer Receipt	BACS	Trade Debtors (1100)		1,235.76	Yes	No	No	Leanne Halsall

From: 31/12/2016 To: 31/01/2017						Justin Timbercrafts Audit Trail Breakdown						20 Jun 2017 16:12	
						Bank Current (1200)	1,235.76			No	No		
						Trade Debtors (1100)	1,235.76			No	No		
						Bank Current (1200)		1,235.76		No	No		
25	20/06/2017	LH	05/01/2017	Happykidz Ltd (HK006)	Customer Receipt	BACS	Trade Debtors (1100)		342.98	No	No	No	Leanne Halsall
							Bank Current (1200)	342.98			No	Yes	
26	20/06/2017	LH	03/01/2017	Toyways plc (TW003)	Customer Receipt	Cheque	Trade Debtors (1100)		1,235.76	No	No	No	Leanne Halsall
							Bank Current (1200)	1,235.76			No	Yes	
27	20/06/2017	LH	04/01/2017	FLW Ltd (FLW002)	Supplier Payment	0012671	Trade Creditors (2100)	923.48		No	No	No	Leanne Halsall
							Bank Current (1200)		923.48		No	Yes	
28	20/06/2017	LH	04/01/2017	Matchsticks Ltd (MCS003)	Supplier Payment	0012672	Trade Creditors (2100)	1,943.26		No	No	No	Leanne Halsall
							Bank Current (1200)		1,943.26		No	Yes	
29	20/06/2017	LH	05/01/2017		Other Payment	Voucher no 10	Petty Cash (1210)		20.00	No	No	No	Leanne Halsall
							Office costs (7500)	20.00			No	No	
30	20/06/2017	LH	05/01/2017		Other Payment	Voucher no 11	Petty Cash (1210)		24.00	No	No	No	Leanne Halsall
							Office costs (7500)	20.00			No	No	
							VAT on Purchases (2201)	4.00			No	No	
31	20/06/2017	LH	01/01/2017		Other Receipt	Cash Sale	Cash Sales (4003)		65.20	No	No	No	Leanne Halsall
							VAT on Sales (2200)		13.04		No	No	
							Bank Current (1200)	78.24			No	Yes	
32	20/06/2017	LH	04/01/2017		Other Receipt	Cash Sale	Cash Sales (4003)		85.25	No	No	No	Leanne Halsall
							VAT on Sales (2200)		17.05		No	No	
							Bank Current (1200)	102.30			No	Yes	
33	20/06/2017	LH	25/01/2017		Journal	JNL01	Drawings (3260)	200.00		No	No	No	Leanne Halsall
							Bank Current (1200)		200.00		No	Yes	

© Copyright Sage (UK) Limited 2018

From: 31/12/2016 To: 31/01/2017						Justin Timbercrafts Audit Trail Breakdown						20 Jun 2017 16:12	
34	20/06/2017	LH	06/01/2017	Funnystuff Ltd (FS001)	Sales QE Invoice	Inv 00303	Sales - Farm Collection (4001)		35.00	No	No	No	Leanne Halsall
							VAT on Sales (2200)		7.00		No	No	
							Trade Debtors (1100)	42.00			No	No	
35	20/06/2017	LH	06/01/2017	Funnystuff Ltd (FS001)	Sales QE Invoice	Inv 00303	Sales - Pets Collection (4002)		45.00	No	No	No	Leanne Halsall
							VAT on Sales (2200)		9.00		No	No	
							Trade Debtors (1100)	54.00			No	No	
36	20/06/2017	LH	06/01/2017	Toyways plc (TW003)	Sales QE Invoice	Inv 00304	Sales - Pets Collection (4002)		270.00	No	No	No	Leanne Halsall
							VAT on Sales (2200)		54.00		No	No	
							Trade Debtors (1100)	324.00			No	No	
37	20/06/2017	LH	08/01/2017	Matchsticks Ltd (MCS003)	Purchase QE Invoice	Inv 3178	Trade Creditors (2100)		1,680.00	No	No	No	Leanne Halsall
							Cost of sales - Materials (5000)	1,400.00			No	No	
							VAT on Purchases (2201)	280.00			No	No	
38	20/06/2017	LH	11/01/2017	Grange Toys Ltd (GRT005)	Purchase QE Invoice	Inv GT2916	Trade Creditors (2100)		672.00	No	No	No	Leanne Halsall
							Cost of sales - Materials (5000)	560.00			No	No	
							VAT on Purchases (2201)	112.00			No	No	
39	20/06/2017	LH	11/01/2017	Happykidz Ltd (HK006)	Customer Receipt	BACS	Trade Debtors (1100)		67.20	No	No	No	Leanne Halsall
							Trade Debtors (1100)		108.00		No	No	
							Trade Debtors (1100)	16.80			No	No	
							Bank Current (1200)	158.40			No	Yes	
40	20/06/2017	LH	11/01/2017	Willow Works Ltd (WWW002)	Supplier Payment	0012674	Trade Creditors (2100)	288.29		No	No	No	Leanne Halsall
							Bank Current (1200)		288.29		No	No	
41	20/06/2017	LH	14/01/2017	Grange Toys Ltd (GRT005)	Supplier Payment	0012675	Trade Creditors (2100)	3,000.00		No	No	No	Leanne Halsall
							Bank Current (1200)		3,000.00		No	Yes	

© Copyright Sage (UK) Limited 2018

From: 31/12/2016
To: 31/01/2017

Justin Timbercrafts
Audit Trail Breakdown

20 Jun 2017
16:12

42	20/06/2017	LH	14/01/2017	Dornley Evening Chronicle (DEC004)	Supplier Payment	0012676	Trade Creditors (2100)	156.00		No	No	No	Leanne Halsall
							Bank Current (1200)		156.00		No	No	
46	20/06/2017	LH	14/01/2017		Other Payment	Voucher no 13	Petty Cash (1210)		10.20	No	No	No	Leanne Halsall

Who: Leanne Halsall   Produced by Sage One   Page 7 of 9

From: 31/12/2016
To: 31/01/2017

Justin Timbercrafts
Audit Trail Breakdown

20 Jun 2017
16:12

							Office costs (7500)	8.50			No	No	
							VAT on Purchases (2201)	1.70			No	No	
47	20/06/2017	LH	14/01/2017		Journal	TRF01	Bank Current (1200)	10,000.00		No	No	Yes	Leanne Halsall
							Bank Loan (1230)		10,000.00		No	No	
48	20/06/2017	LH	14/01/2017		Other Payment	Voucher no 14	Petty Cash (1210)		25.00	No	No	No	Leanne Halsall
							Office costs (7500)	20.83			No	No	
							VAT on Purchases (2201)	4.17			No	No	
51	20/06/2017	LH	18/01/2017		Other Payment	Monthly Rent	Bank Current (1200)		400.00	No	No	Yes	Leanne Halsall
							Rent and rates (7100)	400.00			No	No	
							VAT on Purchases (2201)				No	No	
62	20/06/2017	LH	20/01/2017		Journal	JNL02	Insurance (7610)	150.00		No	No	No	Leanne Halsall
							Repairs and renewals (7800)		150.00		No	No	
63	20/06/2017	LH	31/01/2017		Bank Transfer	TRF02	Bank Current (1200)		94.00	No	No	Yes	Leanne Halsall
							Petty Cash (1210)	94.00			No	No	
64	20/06/2017	LH	09/01/2017		Other Payment	0012673	Bank Current (1200)		250.00	No	No	Yes	Leanne Halsall
							IT Equipment (0030)	208.33			No	No	
							VAT on Purchases (2201)	41.67			No	No	
65	20/06/2017	LH	28/01/2017		Bank Payment	Bank Charge	Bank Current (1200)		32.00	No	No	Yes	Leanne Halsall
							Bank charges and interest (7900)	32.00			No	No	
66	20/06/2017	LH	12/01/2017		Other Payment	Voucher no 12	Petty Cash (1210)		14.80	No	No	No	Leanne Halsall
							Travel and Entertainment (7400)	14.80			No	No	
							VAT on Purchases (2201)				No	No	
67	20/06/2017	LH	28/01/2017		Other Payment	Monthly Rates	Bank Current (1200)		120.00	No	No	Yes	Leanne Halsall
							Rent and rates (7100)	120.00			No	No	
							VAT on Purchases (2201)				No	No	

Task 23 Aged Creditors Report

Aged Creditors Report ⊚

This report shows all outstanding or unallocated supplier transactions, broken down by the ageing periods specified in Record and Transactions Settings.

Sort by Name | | | Q Type to search | To 31/01/2017 📅 | Detailed | Export ▾

Supplier	Credit limit	O/S Amt	< 30 days	< 60 days	< 90 days	< 120 days	Older
Grange Toys Ltd (GRT005)	£10,000.00	£3,221.50	£1,944.00	£1,277.50	£0.00	£0.00	£0.00
Matchsticks Ltd (MCS003)	£5,000.00	£1,680.00	£1,680.00	£0.00	£0.00	£0.00	£0.00
Willow Works Ltd (WWW002)	£8,500.00	£288.00	£288.00	£0.00	£0.00	£0.00	£0.00
	TOTAL	£5,189.50	£3,912.00	£1,277.50	£0.00	£0.00	£0.00

Task 23 Aged Debtors Report

Aged Debtors Report ⊚

This report shows all outstanding or unallocated customer transactions, broken down by the ageing periods specified in Record and Transactions Settings.

Sort by Name | | | Q Type to search | To 31/01/2017 📅 | Detailed | Export ▾

Customer	Credit limit	O/S Amt	< 30 days	< 60 days	< 90 days	< 120 days	Older
Funnystuff Ltd (FS001)	£1,000.00	£96.00	£96.00	£0.00	£0.00	£0.00	£0.00
Happykidz Ltd (HK006)	£8,000.00	£120.00	£120.00	£0.00	£0.00	£0.00	£0.00
Perfect Pastimes Ltd (PP002)	£15,000.00	£13,209.34	£0.00	£13,209.34	£0.00	£0.00	£0.00
Prettypops Ltd (PP004)	£5,000.00	£190.87	£0.00	£190.87	£0.00	£0.00	£0.00
Toyways plc (TW003)	£5,000.00	£474.00	£474.00	£0.00	£0.00	£0.00	£0.00
	TOTAL	£14,090.21	£690.00	£13,400.21	£0.00	£0.00	£0.00

Task 23 Nominal activity – Bank Current Account and Petty Cash (Cash in Hand)

Justin Timbercrafts

Detailed Nominal Activity: Current (1200)

31 December, 2015 - 31 January, 2016

Transaction Type: All

Opening Balance: 0.00 Cr

Closing Balance: 14,713.97 Dr

Trx No	Date	Invoice Number	Name	Type	Reference	Description	Debit	Credit
68	28/01/2016			Bank Payment	Bank Charge			32.00
67	09/01/2016			Other Payment	Cheque 0012673			250.00
66	31/01/2016			Bank Transfer	TFR02			94.00
59	28/01/2016		Domley Evening Chronicle (DEC004)	Other Payment	SOR02			120.00
52	18/01/2016			Other Payment	SOR01			400.00
45	14/01/2016			Bank Transfer	TRF01		10,000.00	
42	14/01/2016		Domley Evening Chronicle (DEC004)	Supplier Payment	Cheque 0012676			156.00
41	14/01/2016		Grange Toys Ltd (GRT005)	Supplier Payment	Cheque 0012675			3,000.00
40	11/01/2016		Willow Works Ltd (WWW002)	Supplier Payment	Cheque ~12674			288.29
39	11/01/2016		Happykidz Ltd (HK006)	Customer Receipt	BACS		158.40	
33	25/01/2016			Journal	JNL01			200.00
32	01/01/2016			Other Receipt	Cash Sale		162.38	
31	01/01/2016			Other Receipt	Cash Sale		78.94	
27	01/01/2016		Kidskidz Ltd (KID000)	Supplier Payment	Cheque 0012672			1,953.23
26	04/01/2016		FLW Ltd (FLW002)	Supplier Payment	Cheque 0012671			923.46
25	05/01/2016		Happykidz Ltd (HK006)	Customer Receipt	BACS		342.98	
24	03/01/2016		Toyways Plc (TW003)	Customer Receipt	Cheque		1,235.76	
12	01/01/2016			Bank Transfer	TRF01			1,000.00
9	31/12/2015			Bank Opening Balance			11,203.30	

Justin Timbercrafts

Detailed Nominal Activity: Petty Cash (1210)

31 December, 2015 - 31 January, 2016

Transaction Type: All

Opening Balance: 0.00 Cr

Closing Balance: 150.00 Dr

Trx No	Date	Invoice Number	Name	Type	Reference	Description	Debit	Credit
66	31/01/2016			Bank Transfer	TFR02		94.00	
50	14/01/2016			Other Payment	Voucher 14			25.00
49	14/01/2016			Other Payment	Voucher 13			10.20
48	12/01/2016			Other Payment	Voucher 12			14.80
47	05/01/2016			Other Payment	Voucher 11			24.00
46	05/01/2016			Other Payment	Voucher 10			20.00
10	31/12/2015			Bank Opening Balance			150.00	

Task 23 Current Account – Bank Reconciliation

Justin Timbercrafts

Justin Timbercrafts

27 West Lane, Dornley, DN22 4RD, United Kingdom
Telephone: 07809 123041
VAT NumberGB 123456789

Bank Account Current (1200)

Statement Date 31/01/2016

Reference Statement 819

Reconciled By Leanne Halsall

Date	Reference	Name	Category	Paid	Received
31/12/2015			Bank Opening Balance	0.00	11,203.30
01/01/2016	TRF01		Transfer: Deposit Account	1,000.00	0.00
03/01/2016	Cheque	Toyways Plc	Customer Receipt	0.00	1,235.76
05/01/2016	BACS	Happykidz Ltd	Customer Receipt	0.00	342.98
04/01/2016	Cheque 0012671	FLW Ltd	Supplier Payment	923.46	0.00
04/01/2016	Cheque 0012672	Matchsticks Ltd	Supplier Payment	1,943.26	0.00
01/01/2016	Cash Sale		Other Receipt	0.00	78.24
04/01/2016	Cash Sale		Other Receipt	0.00	102.30
25/01/2016	JNL01		Journal	200.00	0.00
11/01/2016	BACS	Happykidz Ltd	Customer Receipt	0.00	158.40
14/01/2016	Cheque 0012675	Grange Toys Ltd	Supplier Payment	3,000.00	0.00
14/01/2016	TRF01		Transfer: Business Loan	0.00	10,000.00
18/01/2016	SOR01		Other Payment	400.00	0.00
28/01/2016	SOR02	Dornley Evening Chronicle	Other Payment	120.00	0.00
31/01/2016	TFR02		Transfer: Petty Cash	94.00	0.00
09/01/2016	Cheque 0012673		Other Payment	250.00	0.00
28/01/2016	Bank Charge		Bank Payment	32.00	0.00

Total Received 23,120.98

Total Paid 7,962.72

Starting Balance 0.00

Statement End Balance 15,158.26

Reconciled Balance 15,158.26

Difference 0.00

INDEX

A

Accounting documents, 4
Amending data, 140, 144

B

Bank
    activity, 98
    reconciliation, 116
    reports, 133
    transactions, 86
    transfers, 101

C

Cash transactions, 70
Checking bank activity, 98
Coding, 5
Computerised system, 3
Control accounts, 58
Correction of errors, 110
Creating a password, 144
Credit
    purchases, 83
    sales, 71
    transactions, 70
Customer
    credit notes, 77
    data, 44, 46
    data reports, 51
    receipts, 95
    reports, 125
    statements, 81

D

Discounts received, 29
Double entry, 3

F

Financial year, 12

I

Installing SAGE, 10

M

Making payments, 87

N

Nominal
    codes, 56, 59, 65
    ledger, 56

P

Passwords, 8
Payment
    by BACS and cheque, 87
    of salaries and wages, 70
Petty cash, 70, 103
Producing credit notes, 77

R

Rebuild data, 140
Receipts
    by BACS and cheque, 93
    from customers, 95
Recording receipts, 93
Recurring payment, 136
Risks – computerised systems, 6

S

Setting up the company, 13
Supplier(s), 30
    credit notes, 85
    data reports, 36
    details, 32
    reports, 130

T

Transfers, 101

Trial balance, 67

V

Virus threats, 6

Y

Year end adjustments, 110